SOLDIERS OF FORTUNE

TIME
LIFE ®
BOOKS

Other Publications:

YOUR HOME
THE ENCHANTED WORLD
THE KODAK LIBRARY OF CREATIVE PHOTOGRAPHY
GREAT MEALS IN MINUTES
THE CIVIL WAR
PLANET EARTH
COLLECTOR'S LIBRARY OF THE CIVIL WAR
THE GOOD COOK
THE SEAFARERS
WORLD WAR II
HOME REPAIR AND IMPROVEMENT
THE OLD WEST

For information on and a full description of any of the Time-Life Books
series listed above, please write:

Reader Information
Time-Life Books
541 North Fairbanks Court
Chicago, Illinois 60611

*This volume is one of a series that traces the adventure and
science of aviation, from the earliest manned balloon ascension
through the era of jet flight.*

SOLDIERS OF FORTUNE

by Sterling Seagrave

AND THE EDITORS OF TIME-LIFE BOOKS

TIME-LIFE BOOKS, ALEXANDRIA, VIRGINIA

Time-Life Books Inc.
is a wholly owned subsidiary of

TIME INCORPORATED

FOUNDER: Henry R. Luce 1898-1967

Editor-in-Chief: Henry Anatole Grunwald
President: J. Richard Munro
Chairman of the Board: Ralph P. Davidson
Corporate Editor: Jason McManus
Group Vice President, Books: Reginald K. Brack Jr.
Vice President, Books: George Artandi

TIME-LIFE BOOKS INC.

EDITOR: George Constable
Executive Editor: George Daniels
Editorial General Manager: Neal Goff
Director of Design: Louis Klein
Editorial Board: Dale M. Brown, Roberta Conlan,
Ellen Phillips, Gerry Schremp, Gerald Simons,
Rosalind Stubenberg, Kit van Tulleken, Henry Woodhead
Director of Research: Phyllis K. Wise
Director of Photography: John Conrad Weiser

PRESIDENT: William J. Henry
Senior Vice President: Christopher T. Linen
Vice Presidents: Stephen L. Bair, Robert A. Ellis,
John M. Fahey Jr., Juanita T. James, James L. Mercer,
Joanne A. Pello, Paul R. Stewart, Christian Strasser

THE EPIC OF FLIGHT

Editorial Staff for *Soldiers of Fortune*
Editor: Jim Hicks
Designer: Donald S. Komai
Chief Researcher: W. Mark Hamilton
Picture Editor: Marion F. Briggs
Text Editor: Russell B. Adams Jr.
Staff Writers: Kevin D. Armstrong, Glenn Martin McNatt,
David Thomson
Researchers: Roxie France, Dominick A. Pisano (principals),
Betty Ajemian, LaVerle Berry, Melba Lajara
Assistant Designer: Van W. Carney
Copy Coordinators: Elizabeth Graham, Anthony K. Pordes
Picture Coordinator: Betsy Donahue
Editorial Assistant: Stafford Levon Battle
Art Assistant: Anne K. DuVivier

Editorial Operations
Design: Ellen Robling (assistant director)
Copy Room: Diane Ullius
Editorial Operations: Caroline A. Boubin (manager)
Production: Celia Beattie
Quality Control: James J. Cox (director), Sally Collins
Library: Louise D. Forstall

Correspondents: Elisabeth Kraemer-Singh (Bonn); Margot
Hapgood, Dorothy Bacon (London); Miriam Hsia, Susan
Jonas, Lucy T. Voulgaris (New York); Maria Vincenza Aloisi,
Josephine du Brusle (Paris); Ann Natanson (Rome). Valuable
assistance was also provided by: Carolyn Montserrat
(Barcelona); Martha Mader (Bonn); Enid Farmer (Boston);
Brigid Grauman (Brussels); Katrina van Duyn (Copenhagen);
Lance Keyworth (Helsinki); Marlin Levin (Jerusalem); Judy
Aspinall, Lesley Coleman, Jeremy Lawrence, Karin B.
Pearce, Millicent Trowbridge (London); Cheryl Crooks (Los
Angeles); Trini Bandres (Madrid); Laura Lopez (Mexico
City); Carolyn T. Chubet, Christina Lieberman (New York);
M. T. Hirschkoff (Paris); Mimi Murphy (Rome); Janet Zich
(San Francisco); Mary Johnson (Stockholm).

THE AUTHOR

Sterling Seagrave spent much of his child-
hood in Burma, where his father, Dr. Gordon
Seagrave, won fame as a medical missionary
and as the author of *Burma Surgeon.* As a
freelance journalist, Sterling Seagrave cov-
ered the final months of the Cuban revolution
and later returned to Asia, where he wrote for
several American magazines. He is a former
writer-editor of Time-Life Books.

THE CONSULTANTS for *Soldiers of Fortune*

Tom D. Crouch is Curator of Aeronautics
at the National Air and Space Museum in
Washington, D.C. He holds a Ph.D. from
Ohio State University and is the author of
several books and numerous articles on the
history of aviation.

John F. Guilmartin Jr. is a lieutenant colonel
in the United States Air Force and a special-
ist in military history. He is editor of the *Air
University Review,* the professional journal
of the United States Air Force, and he lec-
tures on military tactics and technology at
the Air War College and the Air Command
and Staff College.

THE CONSULTANTS for *The Epic of Flight*

Charles Harvard Gibbs-Smith, Research Fellow at the Science Museum, London, and
a Keeper-Emeritus of the Victoria and Albert Museum, London, has written or edited
some 20 books and numerous articles on
aeronautical history. In 1978 he served as the
first Lindbergh Professor of Aerospace History at the National Air and Space Museum,
Smithsonian Institution, Washington.

Dr. Hidemasa Kimura, honorary professor at
Nippon University, Tokyo, is the author of
numerous books on the history of aviation
and is a widely known authority on aeronautical engineering and aircraft design. One
plane that he designed established a world
distance record in 1938.

Library of Congress Cataloguing in Publication Data
Seagrave, Sterling
   Soldiers of fortune.
   (Epic of flight)
   Bibliography: p.
   Includes index.
   1. Air pilots, Military — History. 2. Soldiers of fortune —
History — 20th century. 3. Mercenary troops — History —
20th century.   I. Time-Life Books.   II. Title.   III.
Series: Epic of flight.
UG632.S56   358.4'14'0922   81-13599
ISBN 0-8094-3327-3   AACR2
ISBN 0-8094-3326-5 (lib. bdg.)
ISBN 0-8094-3325-7 (retail ed.)

CONTENTS

High fliers who founded the mercenary's trade

As the footloose fliers of John Moisant's aerial circus were barnstorming across the southwestern United States in February 1911, they intended only to perform their usual repertoire of daredevil aerobatic stunts. Instead, they became the world's first flying soldiers of fortune, unwitting founders of a long-lived trade that would continue to attract pilots as colorful and flamboyant as they themselves.

When the Moisant troupe arrived in El Paso, Texas, Mexican rebels were camped just across the Rio Grande, and the Mexican government hired the pilots to scout their positions from the air. René Simon, a dashing Frenchman, made the first flight—preceding by eight months the earliest known wartime mission by a military aviator—and he and other pilots fed reports to the Mexican Army for several days. They faced few dangers and saw their military missions as mere adjuncts to their air-show antics. But those who followed them in the mercenary calling, flying for other countries and in more heated wars, would find that they had embarked on a deadly serious business.

John Moisant wings past the Statue of Liberty on a poster that promotes his air show—which was "international" because its aviators came from four nations.

A Moisant pilot stages a mock attack on United States Army artillery in a San Antonio performance shortly before the show went to El Paso.

Simon's rickety Blériot soars above an arroyo that shelters livestock and men commanded by the Mexican insurgent leader Pascual Orozco.

The show's top daredevil, René Simon—
billed as the Fool Flyer—stands by a Blériot
monoplane that was used to scout rebel
camps near the Mexican town of Juárez.

With René Simon's fellow Frenchman
Roland Garros at the controls, a Blériot lifts
off on another scouting flight. To ensure
a friendly reception should they be downed,
the pilots dropped cigarettes and oranges
to the Mexican rebels. The rebels apparently
appreciated the gifts and the free air shows
and refrained from firing at the planes.

Garros tinkers with his Blériot between flights. His Gallic pride was wounded later when an American member of the Moisant troupe, Charles Hamilton— rather than Garros' friend and compatriot, René Simon—was credited with being the first to fly over an actual scene of war.

In Monterrey, Mexico, shortly after making a series of pioneering observation flights over rebel positions,

pilot René Simon accepts congratulations from Mexican President Porfirio Díaz, whose government fell to the insurgents just three months later.

1

Warriors for hire: a new breed of aerial adventurers

Wobbling like an airborne straw hat over the Greek mountain-lake town of Ioannina on February 8, 1913, the flimsy wood-and-fabric biplane looked incapable of inflicting warlike damage. But the Greeks, aided by their Serbian and Bulgarian allies, were battling with the Ottoman Turks, seeking to drive them out of the Balkans, and this little flying machine was on a daring bombing mission against the Turkish forces holding Fort Bezhani, next to the town. At the controls of the French-built plane, flying in the service of Bulgaria, was an audacious Russian pilot who would be known to history only as N. de Sakoff.

Most of the aviators who flew against the Turks in this conflict restricted their work to reconnaissance, reporting on enemy troop deployments and scouting artillery targets. But the aircraft at their disposal were generally so decrepit that pilots considered themselves lucky to return alive even from such noncombat assignments. Only the fearless Sakoff and a countryman named Kolchin were foolhardy enough to attempt bombing runs with their makeshift warplanes.

On this raid, Sakoff, perching on a wooden seat in front of the noisy engine, carried six small bombs tied with stout cord to his heavily booted feet. The few details available from scanty accounts of the raid indicate that Sakoff's feet protruded beyond the lower wing's leading edge, with the bombs resting beside them on the wing, three to a side. That way, as he approached Fort Bezhani, he could let one bomb down gently on its cord to swing from his right foot and another from the left, both of them suspended between the plane's skilike landing runners. A sharp jerk of Sakoff's feet was all that would be required to release the slipknots and let the bombs fall free. The main problem was altitude. If he was to be reasonably certain of hitting the target, he had to fly below 500 feet, which put him in range of ground fire.

As he neared the walls of Fort Bezhani, the Turkish defenders greeted him with a barrage of angry gunfire. Two bullets ripped through the biplane's wings, but Sakoff ignored them and forged onward over the walls. He probably made three passes over the fort, jerking his feet to

Two American mercenaries on opposing sides, Dean Ivan Lamb in a Curtiss biplane (foreground) and Phil Rader in a Christofferson, jockey for position to fire their pistols at each other over Mexico in 1913, in what is thought to be the world's first dogfight.

free two of the crude bombs each time. Below him, he could see that his attack was causing a panic among the Turks in the garrison.

After letting loose his last two bombs, Sakoff banked and headed away through a storm of ground fire. But as he droned toward his home base at Nicopolis, about an hour's flying time to the south, he discovered that the Turks had managed to do more than punch a few holes through his wing. Suddenly, the little plane's engine coughed and died, and when the Russian aviator turned to inspect the fuel tank, mounted above and behind him, he saw that it had been shot through by an enemy bullet and had drained dry.

Sakoff managed to nurse his plane down near Preveza, on the coast of the Ionian Sea. There, with the help of local Greek residents, he repaired the damaged tank, refueled and was on his way with only a modest delay. When he landed again at Nicopolis, he told of his bombardment and described the poor state of Fort Bezhani's defenses. The Greek military authorities were inspired to attack, and Ioannina was in their hands a few days later.

The man to whom the Greeks owed their victory belonged to a special breed of warrior-aviators. Unlike the Turks, who opposed him, or the Bulgarians, for whom he flew his remarkably successful mission, Sakoff was not motivated by patriotism. He was a mercenary combat pilot, flying for money in a strange land. He and his compatriot Kolchin were among the first in a long line of aerial soldiers of fortune who chose to make a living fighting in somebody else's war.

Soldiers of fortune got into the business of air war at the very beginning, at about the same time that the military organizations of the world's major nations began to explore the uses of airplanes for combat. When Sakoff dropped his bombs, aviation was still in its infancy. The Wright brothers had made their first powered flight just 10 years earlier, and during that decade flying machines had been regarded primarily as sporting objects or experimental devices. Sakoff's attack on Fort Bezhani was, in fact, one of the earliest air raids in history. (The first recorded instance of bombs being dropped from an airplane in combat had occurred only two years before, in 1911, during a brief war between Italy and Turkey in North Africa; on that occasion, too, the Turks had been the targets. An intrepid Italian officer reconnoitering the enemy lines from a sports plane took the opportunity to toss four tiny hand-held bombs at his startled foe.)

Some weeks after Sakoff's raid, Kolchin earned an even more notable distinction in the history of aerial warfare, although one that he undoubtedly would rather have forgone. Attempting a similar low-level bombing run, he was shot down and killed by Turkish ground fire, thus becoming the first aviator ever to die in air combat.

If anyone had told Sakoff and Kolchin or the many air mercenaries who came after them that they were carrying on a historic tradition going back to the Renaissance and its companies of mercenary soldiers called *condottieri,* to medieval knights-errant who offered their services

for hire or lent them in the cause of justice or honor, and even to the many mercenaries among the heroes of ancient Greece, the pilots would have laughed or been embarrassed. But in fact they were the heirs to those earlier soldiers of fortune and were impelled by the same motives. They flew for money, and the loyalty of most of them lasted only as long as their employers paid them. But for some, money was not the main object; a large proportion of the foreign mercenary pilots who flew for the Republican side during the Spanish Civil War were idealists who went into battle for a cause, although they were paid well. While many of the pilots who spent their lives ducking bullets in obscure wars and remote revolutions were warriors by trade, others were simply adventurers who loved to fly and who would take on almost any flying job that called for daring and unusual skill.

Wanderlust and aviation were about the only things that aerial mercenaries did have in common. Among them were misfits, rogues, renegades and honest, well-educated gentlemen, alcoholics, ne'er-do-wells and scions of patrician families, romantics and chronic liars, altruists and swindlers, frauds, geniuses, and perhaps even an occasional psychopath. Sometimes one aviator qualified for several of these categories. One misfit-genius was Claire Chennault, a stunt pilot turned combat tactician who found it impossible to sell his radical ideas for the use of fighter aircraft to his own nation's military leaders. But he was later vindicated by the achievements of his band of mercenaries, the Flying Tigers, over the jungles and rice paddies of Burma and China. Chennault believed that the mercenary often had a vital role to play, and he never tired of repeating A. E. Housman's poem, "Epitaph on an Army of Mercenaries":

> These, in the day when heaven was falling,
> The hour when earth's foundations fled,
> Followed their mercenary calling,
> Took their wages and are dead.
>
> Their shoulders held the sky suspended:
> They stood and earth's foundations stay.
> What God abandoned these defended
> And saved the sum of things for pay.

Paid they all were, in one form of currency or another. And more than once they "saved the sum of things," sometimes on behalf of a major power that hired them when involvement of its own military air arm would have offended international law or morality, at other times for a weak, threatened government that could not afford its own air force. There were other occasions when air mercenaries worked not to save the sum of things but to overthrow it—flying for revolutionary movements. No matter who was paying them, however, few air adventurers made their fortunes flying, and those who did soon lost them. But they were wealthy in their knowledge of things beyond the experience of most men, and the legends they created—from the Balkan Wars of 1912-1913 through the fall of Saigon in 1975—would enrich and enliven the history of aviation.

During the decade after Sakoff's daring bombing raid on Fort Bezhani, the trade of the flying soldier of fortune developed as rapidly as did the use of airplanes in combat. Mercenary pilots fought for (and against) revolutionary armies in Mexico, hired themselves out to France to fight the Germans in World War I, attacked Berber horsemen in North Africa and helped the Polish Army invade the Soviet Union in 1920. In the beginning their planes were frail marvels of wood, wire and cloth—box-kite-shaped Farmans, Wrights and Voisins, or birdlike Taubes, Blériots and Nieuports. In such primitive craft they pioneered techniques of aerial warfare—including the use of firearms for air-to-air combat and the use of bombsights—years before the first effective military air services took up the same innovations in World War I.

But they were noted not so much for their contributions to the science of war (which were, for the most part, crude if ingenious, and rarely developed to perfection) as they were for the romantic public image they established almost as soon as they took to the skies. They were envied and admired as dashing heroes who made their fortunes out of thin air, zooming high above the bloody battlefields, touching down only long enough to hug the ladies, pour whiskey into the fuel tank and rebuckle their Sam Browne belts—or so the legends, which were generated mainly by the mercenaries themselves, made it appear.

At about the same time that Sakoff was mounting his raid in the Balkans, some of those legends began to take shape half a world away among other pilots who were drifting down to join the Mexican Revolution. It was a chaotic moment in Mexican history. The long-entrenched regime of President Porfirio Díaz had been overthrown in 1911 and replaced first by the reformer Francisco Madero, then by the usurper Victoriano Huerta. In the countryside, Pancho Villa, Emiliano Zapata and other leaders of revolutionary bands joined forces behind General Venustiano Carranza to unseat the reactionary Huerta. To American and European pilots, unschooled in Mexican politics, the rapid succession of leaders and rebels took on a comic-opera confusion that was kept straight only by lumping the rivals into two factions: the Federal government forces, or *federales,* and the rebels.

Some of the foreign pilots who went to Mexico were openly seeking excitement, danger and easy money, and they found all three in large measure. Others, such as John Hector Worden—an American who flew for the *federales*—became mercenaries almost by accident. But before he was finished, Worden had become known as the world's first expert in the use of aircraft against guerrilla forces.

Born in New York City in 1885, Worden was a Cherokee Indian and was educated at the Carlisle Indian School in Pennsylvania. Later, on a visit to France, he became so excited about aviation that he took flying lessons at the Blériot school in Étampes. Returning to Manhattan in 1911, he polished his skills at the Moisant Aviation School in Garden City, Long Island, and soon found employment as an instructor in Galveston, Texas. Airplane manufacturers were eager to sell their wares to anyone they could induce to go aloft, and the best way to create interest in aviation was to sponsor flying exhibitions at fairgrounds— which they did, from coast to coast. After signing on as an exhibition flier for the aggressive Moisant company, Worden was sent to Mexico City to demonstrate planes for the *federales.* Enthusiastic Mexican Army officers, eager to find military uses for these delightful machines, persuaded Worden to fly some aerial patrols and scouting missions against the rebels.

The hazards might have daunted a lesser man. There were no airfields or trained ground crews. Gasoline was of poor quality and caused frequent engine trouble. Worse still, rebel soldiers took frequent pot

American aviator John Hector Worden (third from right), stands with his aircraft and ground crew at the Mexican front in 1912.

shots at Worden's aircraft. But with the honorary rank of captain in the Federal Army, he stuck to his assignment with singular dedication. By the time he returned to the United States at the end of 1912, he had gained sufficient experience in antiguerrilla air war to hold forth on the subject in the New York journal *Aircraft*—whose editors billed him as "the first and only aviator up to the present time to participate in actual warfare in the Western hemisphere." The appellation was slightly erroneous, taking no account of a group of barnstormers who had flown reconnaissance missions for the Mexican government the year before *(pages 6-13)*.

Worden's carefully reasoned article appeared in *Aircraft's* December 1912 issue. It noted that the difficult Mexican terrain, with its many dry riverbeds that became roaring torrents during heavy rains, made the vital, single-track railway system unusually vulnerable to sabotage. A handful of rebels could easily burn a railroad bridge and escape to the nearby mountains. It was impossible to station soldiers all along the tracks: To do so, Worden observed wryly, "would require more than the standing army of Germany." But when the government sent escorts with every train, the troops often discovered that the bridges had already been destroyed, or they blundered into enemy ambushes. If they pursued the rebels, they were led into the hills to their doom, leaving the train to the mercy of other rebels.

To Worden, airplanes were the only solution. "What could be more simple or easy," he wrote, "than for an aviator to start out ahead of the train, fly over the track and reconnoitre the threatened district, and report in time for the train to turn back?" Special troops could then be dispatched to protect the bridge and chase the rebels into the hills.

Worden, seen here proudly wearing the uniform of the Mexican Federal Army, became an eloquent advocate of military aviation after his experiences as a mercenary pilot in the Mexican Revolution.

Mexican rebels prepare to ambush a Federal train—a tactic that Worden argued could be easily foiled by reconnaissance flights.

Unfortunately for the *federales,* the rebels also recognized the value of military aviation. And both sides in the Mexican conflict soon went beyond aerial observation and began tinkering with the idea of hurling bombs at each other from the air, although Worden had cautioned that it was unreasonable to expect a flier to throw bombs down with any accuracy, since aviators had never been trained for such duty. Then a French-born American pilot named Didier Masson arrived as a mercenary for the rebels.

Masson had been a mechanic for the pioneer French aviator Louis Paulhan on an exhibition tour of the United States in 1910. He had liked America and stayed to begin barnstorming on his own. When two Mexican rebel colonels on a recruiting trip met with Masson in Los Angeles early in 1913, he was an instructor at the Glenn L. Martin flying school in nearby Balboa. The Mexicans offered him $300 a month base pay, plus $50 for each reconnaissance flight and $250 for every bombing run. As hungry for adventure as he was for money, Masson threw in his lot with the revolution. The colonels bought a $5,000 Martin pusher plane for Masson to use. It had a 75-horsepower Curtiss engine and could fly 100 miles carrying a passenger and 150 pounds of bombs.

The new plane, christened the *Sonora,* was trucked to the Mexican border near Nogales, Arizona, by Masson's resourceful mechanic, Thomas J. Dean—who was then stopped by a sheriff who rightly suspected that the aircraft was bound for Mexico without benefit of customs formalities. The sheriff went off to get help, leaving a one-legged deputy named Hopkins to stand guard over Dean and the flying machine; after some persuasion Deputy Hopkins gave in to a bribe. "He was bought over," Didier Masson wrote later with Gallic aplomb, "and came with the truck to Hermosillo.'' Later, according to Masson, the Mexicans made Hopkins a major in their revolutionary army.

The rebels at this time were strong only in the northwestern state of Sonora and were trying to advance down a rail line from the Arizona border to the Federal base at Guaymas on the Gulf of California. The base was cut off from overland reinforcement, but three gunboats, the *Guerrero,* the *Morelos* and the *Tampico,* protected the port so stoutly that Guaymas was able to repulse the most determined assaults. The only solution, the rebels decided, was to bomb the gunboats into submission from the air.

Since their success now depended on Didier Masson, the rebels made him comfortable some 40 miles from Guaymas at the town of Moreno, where they had optimistically built a permanent airfield. The pilot and his mechanic were housed in a plush Pullman car that was divided into sleeping quarters, dining room and kitchen with an icebox. Masson responded by throwing himself into the task at hand, beginning with a series of reconnaissance flights.

Meanwhile, workers at the rebel rail yards converted the plane to a bomber *(pages 24-25)* by adding an ingenious bombsight and a bomb rack, and mechanic Dean fashioned bombs from sections of iron pipe. Each pipe bomb was packed with sticks of dynamite and steel rivets and had a cap screwed on each end. A detonator rod protruded from the

His cap turned rakishly to the rear, French-born mercenary Didier Masson grips the wheel of the Sonora, which he flew as a bomber for the Mexican insurgents in 1913. Beside him is Gustavo Salinas, nephew of the rebel leader Venustiano Carranza.

nose cap; a safety clip kept the rod from moving until just before the bomb was dropped. At the rear end was another rod holding directional fins. Masson recalled long afterward that eight of these lethal pipe bombs could be fitted into the rack slung underneath the plane, but some aviation historians contend that the aircraft could not have carried more than three of the explosive devices when a bombardier was aboard, since they weighed some 30 pounds apiece. The bombardier pulled a cord, which yanked out the safety clip and simultaneously tugged the bomb from the rack.

Carrying a full load of bombs, Masson and his Mexican bombardier-observer, Captain Joaquin Alcalde, took off on May 30, 1913, for their first combat raid—and the world's first aerial bomb attack on a vessel of war. The gunboat crewmen fired at the Sonora with gusto, but they did not once hit the plane. The pilot and bombardier fared little better. Flying at an altitude of 2,500 feet, they placed their bombs all around the Guerrero but managed only to splash its deck with water.

Masson and Alcalde tried again the next day. This time they had the satisfaction of watching the frightened sailors leaping overboard, but again they failed to hit any of the craft. Returning to the airfield, Masson resumed experiments. He made a number of adjustments to the bomb fins and the sight but again failed to hit the Guaymas gunboats. On the next attempt, Masson crashed on takeoff and had to wait four weeks while replacement parts were smuggled from the United States.

When the Sonora was airworthy again, Masson and Alcalde resumed the attacks on the gunboats. On their first pass a trial bomb fell very close to the Guerrero, so they circled back and dropped the remainder of the explosives. Not one struck the vessel.

On August 4, Masson tried once more, this time from 2,000 feet, and with Dean in the bombardier's seat. But his bad luck still held. As Dean dropped a test bomb through a barrage of gunfire, the Curtiss engine sputtered and quit. They were over the enemy harbor, and their only hope was to glide across Guaymas Bay and attempt to land inside friendly lines near the town of Empalme. As a precaution, they jettisoned their bombs. Luckily, Masson brought the Sonora down gently—when he climbed out of the plane, he discovered that an unexploded bomb, snagged by its cord, was trailing behind.

The following day, after patching a broken fuel line, Masson and Dean set out for Moreno, only to have their engine break down beyond all repair. When they finally struggled back to their home base, they turned in their resignations.

Not long after Didier Masson's pioneering experiment in aerial bombing, the American mercenary pilot Dean Ivan Lamb blazed another trail when he tangled with a rival mercenary in what may well have been the world's first aerial dogfight.

Lamb appeared in Mexico at about the same time that Didier Masson quit in frustration. A footloose romantic, a chronic drifter and a hopeless teller of exaggerated tales, he had wandered the world as a merchant

Three inches in diameter, the Sonora's
bombs were 18-inch-long iron pipes packed
with dynamite and rivets. A detonator
rod protruded from each bomb's nose.

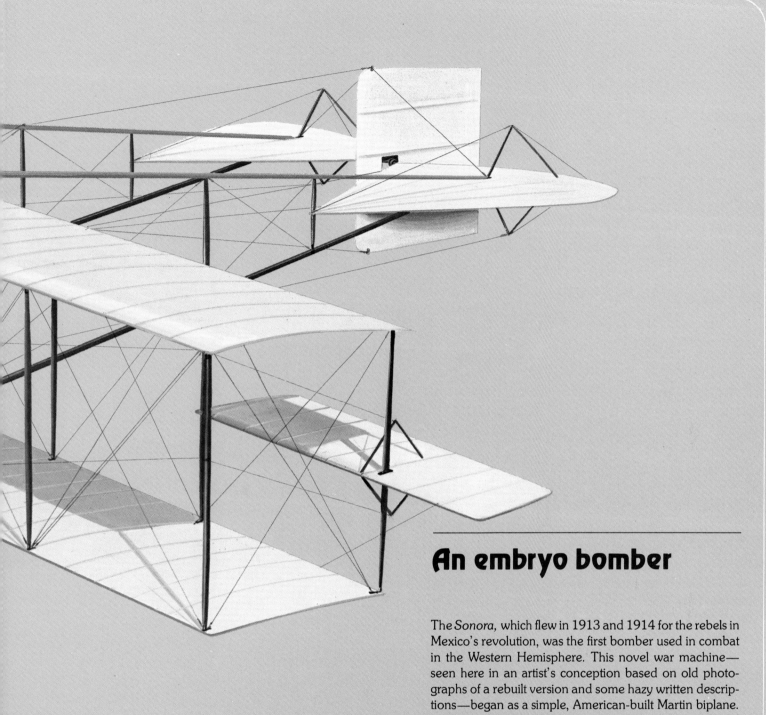

A marvelous tangle of wood, wire and fabric, the Sonora had a wingspan of about 50 feet. Its rear-mounted propeller was powered by a 75-hp Curtiss engine.

An embryo bomber

The *Sonora,* which flew in 1913 and 1914 for the rebels in Mexico's revolution, was the first bomber used in combat in the Western Hemisphere. This novel war machine— seen here in an artist's conception based on old photographs of a rebuilt version and some hazy written descriptions—began as a simple, American-built Martin biplane. It was converted to a warplane by adding a bomb rack and a bombardier's seat.

A crude sight was made from a square and cross wires on a pivoting rod attached to the bombardier's seat. By trial and error, the bombardier could adjust the angle of the sight to the best position for bombing at a given speed and altitude. The bombardier pulled the bombs from their rack by yanking cords, which are not shown becase no adequate description of their placement survives.

The *Sonora's* first victim was confidence in the plane itself. Flown by mercenary Didier Masson, it failed—after five bombing runs—to even hit a Federal gunboat.

sailor until he gave up the sea in 1912 and decided to learn how to fly. When he made his way down to Mexico in the summer of 1913, he was just 27. He almost certainly invented the story of how he confronted Pancho Villa; the yarn was typical of the kind told by early mercenary pilots to make their lives sound glamorous.

As Lamb told it, the bull-like revolutionary had considerable doubts about Lamb's abilities when the young American offered his services as a flier. "So *you* can fly?" Villa supposedly snorted as his men snickered and gathered around to watch the fun. "You are so skinny, the wind she would blow you away." Lamb said Villa then gave him a shove that sent him sprawling into the dirt. He claimed that he sprang to his feet and punched Villa in the moustache, drawing a trickle of blood from the general's lip. Rifles clicked.

"No," Villa ordered. "Enough." He wiped his lip and squinted at Lamb. "All right. You are a flier and fighter, too. The job is yours."

Lamb was soon flying his Curtiss pusher for the revolution. His assignment: to find and destroy the American mercenary Phil Rader, whose Christofferson biplane had been harassing Villa's forces for nearly two months without opposition.

Lamb cruised the sun-baked mountains and shimmering deserts for three days, seeing only turkey buzzards wheeling through the blinding sky. In such terrain a forced landing would mean almost certain death. At last he saw the Christofferson descending on him like a king vulture. There was a revolver in Rader's hand. A bullet ripped through the right wing of Lamb's plane. He pulled back his stick, rising like a box kite caught in an updraft. Drawing his revolver from his holster, Lamb took aim and fired at Rader's whirling propeller. He missed. Side by side, the two cloth-covered flying machines roared through the afternoon. They were so close that Lamb could make out Rader's drooping black moustache. He could also see the snout of Rader's revolver, leveled and blasting. Lamb braced his knees against the controls and fired back. Both men missed their targets.

Lamb circled away to reload, and then the two pilots again swooped, drew alongside each other, yawed, fired and reloaded. Aside from Rader's lucky first shot, not a single bullet struck. At last, their ammunition exhausted, they banked and drew apart, each heading home.

Fortunately for Lamb, the battle had taken place within sight of the rebel-controlled town of Naco, and when Lamb returned to his base he was immediately elevated to the pantheon of heroes of the revolution. Rader, furthermore, did not reappear, probably choosing to continue his money-making sorties in other Mexican skies where he could earn his pay without interference from another mercenary.

Not long after Lamb and Rader introduced firearms to the sky, the Mexican Revolution spawned another major innovation in air warfare. In February of 1914 a 27-year-old American engineer named Lester Barlow, who had left his job with a mining company in Mexico to join Pancho Villa as a volunteer, assembled a logistical wonder he called his "tactical war airplane unit." Barlow's tactical unit was nothing less than a mobile air base on rails—minus only a runway, which could be improvised in the northern Mexican desert almost anywhere the specially equipped train stopped. It was complete with its own locomotive, a machine-shop boxcar, a Pullman sleeping car, a supply boxcar, a magazine car to carry bombs, and flatcars to carry assembled planes and a few automobiles—all guarded by an armored rail car. The train was painted vivid green and decorated with contrasting letters spelling out "Aviation Division of the Army of the North." It was a strange-looking affair, its flatcars loaded with Curtiss, Wright and Christofferson flying machines, along with some nameless hybrids.

Carrying most of Villa's airplanes and many of his troops, the Tactical Unit puffed its way around Northern Mexico to strike at the *federales* wherever they concentrated. Unfortunately for the pilots in Barlow's entourage, not all of Villa's forces knew that the train's aircraft were flying for the revolution. Indeed, American flier Howard Rinehart recalled later that Villa's own troops were frequently more dangerous than were the *federales,* who managed only occasionally to put a bullet through the wing of a passing plane. "Even on the messenger trips," he said, "we were completely surrounded on landing, and on all occasions were lucky not to have been killed by the troops, as they had no knowledge that Villa had a plane and it bore no distinguishing marks."

Despite the efforts of trigger-happy ground troops, only one foreign mercenary pilot—the American exhibition flier Farnum Fish—was brought to grief by gunfire during the Mexican Revolution. Fish was on his very first flight for Pancho Villa, passing at 500 feet over enemy lines within sight of his own airfield, when the *federales* loosed a fusillade at his plane. "It seemed to me," Lester Barlow recalled, "that every Mexican, and there seemed to be thousands of them, opened fire at him. For the few minutes that he was over the troops there was a continuous roar of rifle fire."

Fish urgently pushed his machine into a steeply banked turn and started back toward the rebel lines, where Barlow and others from the Tactical Unit were waiting anxiously. The plane landed safely after a long, flat glide, but as Barlow dashed toward the cockpit he saw that Fish was bleeding profusely and that his aircraft was spattered with blood. Only one bullet had struck him, but it had struck him twice—passing through a fleshy part of his leg before nicking his shoulder. According to Barlow, Fish recovered within a few days and was even able to chuckle about his mishap. But Barlow added: "Apparently, his ambition for war was satisfied, as he returned to his home in Los Angeles."

Farnum Fish seems to have made his way homeward without incident. But the same could not be said for Howard Rinehart who, dissatisfied with his pay schedule and tired of being menaced by supposedly friendly forces, yearned to return to the United States after less than two months in Villa's employ.

Rinehart had been signed up for the Mexican Revolution in March of

1915 by an aviation promoter named J. S. Berger. Rinehart had flown for Berger before, in carelessly run air shows throughout the southern United States, and was somewhat suspicious when Berger presented himself as Pancho Villa's "chief of aircraft." Even after the promoter plunked down cash for one Wright Model B and one Model HS (so called because of its Hispano-Suiza engine), Rinehart remained wary, but he was soon heading for Mexico with a group of other adventure-some barnstormers and exhibition fliers.

The new recruits spent several weeks in Juárez assembling their Model B, but after a high wind swept it across a field and smashed it to pieces, they went on by train to rebel headquarters in Monterrey, taking the crated HS with them. Then Rinehart's suspicions began to deep-en. "Up to this point," he said later, "expense money had been very liberal, but no salaries had been forthcoming." It was just like his old exhibition days with the tightfisted Berger. "There was food to keep the pilots and mechanics working, but talk of salaries was met by promises and conversations. I still had hopes, however, as there was plenty of money in sight." But he was beginning to wonder if Berger was pocketing their pay.

Rinehart learned soon enough of the hazards of military aviation in the Mexican Revolution. His first mission was to carry a message to one of Villa's field commanders; on landing, he had to take cover and wave a white flag to get the soldiers to stop shooting at him. "Apparently," he

With the American pilot Howard Rinehart seated in the cockpit, ground crewmen push out the Wright Model HS plane bought in March 1915 by Pancho Villa, the Mexican rebel leader. Rinehart, an instructor at Orville Wright's flying school, had been hired to fly the plane for the insurgents.

said later, "the temptation of taking a shot at a plane—any plane—was just too much for any Mexican with a rifle to resist."

The salary problem remained unsettled, so Rinehart began claiming engine trouble as an excuse for not flying. Finally, he jumped at a chance to take a message to a general named Rodriguez in Matamoros, near the Texas border. He knew that once he was there, he could hop across the Rio Grande to Brownsville and freedom.

Rinehart was accompanied on the flight by an armed escort, a captain in Villa's army. There had been constant rumors of pilots flying planes over to the enemy in return for large sums of money. Rinehart himself had been approached with offers of as much as $15,000. Suspecting treachery, he had laughed them off. But Villa was taking no chances with his mercenary pilots, especially those who had grievances over back pay.

Nearing Matamoros, Rinehart and his companion could not identify the troops below, so they landed in the mesquite scrub outside town. Rinehart got down, nearly stepping on a coiled rattlesnake, and the two made their way on foot through what they believed to be enemy terrain. While skirting a pond of green scum, they heard voices and dived into the muck to hide behind a log. After scrambling from the pond, they hid in some bushes until dusk, tortured by swarms of mosquitoes. Then Rinehart's Mexican escort squelched in wet shoes to a roadside cantina, only to learn that they had been in friendly territory all along.

They reached General Rodriguez' headquarters at about midnight. Rinehart was desperate now to escape. He was to fly back to Monterrey the next morning, but when he returned to the plane hidden among the mesquite, he tinkered with the engine and insisted on a test flight. The escort went along, his guns protruding ominously from their holsters. With a bit of help from Rinehart, the engine began to sputter, and when he came in for a quick landing he threw the plane into an intentional skid that wrecked one of the wheels. There were no spares or suitable repair facilities in Matamoras, so Rinehart was sent across the border to Brownsville to get the wheel fixed. He did not return.

Howard Rinehart was not alone in his disenchantment. As eager as they were to go to Mexico, most of the foreign pilots who flew for the *federales* and the rebels were, before long, just as eager to leave. Newcomers arrived every month, but the veterans were packing up. They found one excuse or another to escape—with or without pay. But some of them could not shake their taste for the life of a mercenary pilot and promptly made their way to Europe to take part in the air battles of World War I.

Among those who had preceded them to Paris was Weston Bert Hall, one of the most astonishing characters in the annals of aviation and a man without peer in his capacity to invent extraordinary adventures and thereby paint himself as a great hero. Mixing a few facts with considerable fiction, Bert Hall concocted feats of daring that involved him in everything from the Balkan Wars and the Russian Revolution to the command of the Chinese air force.

A few of Hall's closest acquaintances knew him to be a creature of his own contrivance, but he managed to deceive the world at large for decades, being described as the leading air soldier of fortune by no less august a publication than the *New York Times,* taking in even such renowned journalists as Ernie Pyle and having his book of dubious memoirs praised by noted aviation writers. In fact, nobody would ever be certain that Hall was really his name, or where he came from, since he gave his birthplace variously as Higginsville, Missouri, Bowling Green, Kentucky, and El Paso, Texas.

Hall's memoirs, published in 1929 as *One Man's War,* convincingly portrayed the ebullient author as a debonair denizen of the fashionable boulevards of Paris. In fact, Hall had finagled his passage to Paris by getting a job as chauffeur for a Texas millionaire. Once in Paris, he had quit or been fired and was supporting himself by driving a taxi when Great Britain and France went to war against Germany in August of 1914. That month, he and his friend James Bach joined the wealthy William Thaw—who had made a name for himself while he was still a student at Yale by stunt-flying a Curtiss seaplane—and about 40 other Americans in enlisting in the French Foreign Legion. They made up a self-styled American Volunteer Corps, and in the grim closing months of the year they found themselves dug in at the front, fighting an in-

Aviators of the Lafayette Escadrille gather in front of one of their planes during World War I. Founded by Norman Prince (sixth from left) to fight for the French, the unit of American soldiers of fortune went into action for the first time on the Alsatian front.

festation of lice in the freezing, stinking pestilence of the trenches.

It was not long before they began to talk about forming a unit of American volunteer pilots. The French were reluctant to accept untested foreigners in their elite air service, so Thaw, Bach and Hall began glamorizing their careers. Thaw had already invented a military record with the Mexican Army in order to get into the Foreign Legion. Now, although he had flown only the Curtiss seaplane, he began claiming that he could fly almost anything with wings. Bach, a mechanical engineer who had lived most of his life in Paris, also invented an impressive aviation background. And Bert Hall began to concoct the bogus biography that one day would be taken as gospel by a credulous world.

According to Hall, he had studied flying under the fabled pioneer aviators Maurice and Henry Farman in 1910, at Buc, near Paris. He was then hired by the Turkish Sultan to fly in the Balkan War at wages of $100 a day in gold coin. When the Turks were slow to pay him, Hall claimed, he switched sides and went to work flying for the Bulgarians against the Turks, serving at the same time as the Russian mercenaries Sakoff and Kolchin. Then the Bulgarians arrested him because they suspected him of plotting to rejoin the Turkish side, and Hall insisted that he escaped the firing squad only when his trusty mechanic, "Monsieur André Pierce," bribed Hall's way out of the dungeon.

In their effort to fly for France, Thaw, Hall and Bach won the support of Lieutenant Felix Brocard, an influential French aviator and an old friend of Thaw's. Thanks to Brocard's intervention, wheels turned and the three Americans were transferred to flight training.

Hall, for one, did not get off to a good start. Arriving at the air base at Pau, preceded by his fantastic storytelling, he was taken by the commandant to a Blériot monoplane and told to take it up. Hall had never touched aircraft controls before, and now he fell back on raw courage.

"I'll drive this thing like a baby carriage," he said.

The Blériot, with Hall at the controls, then "zigzagged across the field like a drunken duck," according to one amazed observer, and smashed to pieces against a hangar. The furious commandant shouted: "You have never even been in an airplane! But you have guts, that much I'll say for you!" And he allowed Hall to stay. Despite their inexperience, Hall and Bach received their flight commissions in the summer of 1915 and went off to the front. Bill Thaw was already there, having passed his training period with relative ease.

A short time later, the brave but luckless Jimmy Bach crash-landed in enemy territory and was captured. Then in April of 1916, Bill Thaw and Bert Hall were assigned to join their fellow Americans Norman Prince, Elliott Cowdin, Kiffin Rockwell, James McConnell and Victor Chapman as the nucleus of an all-American squadron that would be called the Lafayette Escadrille, after the Marquis de Lafayette, French hero of the American Revolution. They were joined later by Didier Masson, well seasoned by his experiences in Mexico, and a French-born American, Raoul Lufbery, who would become the famous unit's top ace.

From the very beginning, Bert Hall did not fit in. Most of the men who came to fill the growing ranks of the Lafayette Escadrille were young American patricians, well educated and self-assured. Hall was a blowhard who was always trying to play the role of what he called a "gay-dog hero." Understandably, they looked down their noses at him, while he regarded all but a few of them as effete snobs. By their own account they considered him a lying braggart who cheated at cards and picked off aerial kills that had been set up by fellow fighter pilots during dogfights.

Hall's squadronmates soon began to conspire to have him transferred, and on November 1, 1916, he was assigned to a French squadron to fly Nieuports and the recently introduced Spad fighters. By then he had two confirmed kills and blithely claimed a number of other enemy planes shot down either over German lines or out of sight of witnesses from his own side.

Now he was set to embark on adventures of a different kind. According to Hall, before he could settle in with his new squadron he was asked by French intelligence officers to undertake a secret mission to Eastern Europe and Russia. He said they gave him a French passport to travel as part of a trade mission to demonstrate the new Spad. In addition to showing off the new fighter, Hall was to take note of the attitudes and comments of czarist military commanders toward their part in the fight against Germany. He was to report, also, on the violent currents of revolution that were sweeping Russia.

Hall arrived in Petrograd on January 14, 1917. According to his later account, he demonstrated the Spad before military commanders at air bases all the way from Latvia to Rumania. At various points along the way, he said, he shot down marauding German aircraft, bombed an enemy summit meeting in the grand palace of Sofia, Bulgaria, and was decorated by Russia's Czar Nicholas II in a ceremony that Hall described as "positively Medieval and damned impressive." Perhaps more impressive, though, were the revolutionary mobs that Hall observed running through the streets of Petrograd in early March, and he wisely decided to leave Russia as rapidly as possible.

Unable to exit to Scandinavia because of closed borders, he claimed to have struck a bargain with a czarist general to smuggle the general's elderly wife out of Russia on the Trans-Siberian Railway. By the time the two travelers reached Vladivostok the Russian Revolution was in full rampage, Czar Nicholas had abdicated and the Bolsheviks were maneuvering to seize power. It was no time to loiter, and Hall took the general's wife by train to Shanghai and then by ship to Yokohama, Japan. There, said Hall, she sold some of her jewelry and paid him $38,000 for his successful completion of a perilous mission.

Pocketing this princely sum, Hall embarked by ship for the United States. He remained in his own country only briefly—turning down (he said) the offer of a commission in the aviation section of the United States Marine Corps—and then went on to Paris, which he

This 1919 advertisement for a theater in Portland, Oregon, features Bert Hall as the star of a film called A Romance of the Air. After serving in the Lafayette Escadrille, Hall spent time in Hollywood as an actor, writer and consultant on aviation movies.

now regarded as his adopted home. There, outshone by the new flying aces who dominated the headlines, he haunted the bistros for a while before resigning his French commission. Soon he was back in the United States, writing and lecturing to promote himself as "America's famous ace."

Nearly 10 years would pass before Hall reappeared in action on the other side of the globe, widely hailed by then as the world's leading air soldier of fortune. Meanwhile, his fellow knights-errant managed to carry on amazingly well in his absence from the European stage.

In the long months following Bert Hall's escape across Siberia, the Bolsheviks gained absolute power, waged a bloody civil war to wipe out the last pockets of czarist sympathizers and tightened their grip on all of Russia. In Europe, World War I came to an end, and in the confusion of its aftermath the Bolsheviks attempted to extend their Communist dictatorship as far as possible into the West. A primary target was Poland,

Seven of the eight American mercenary fliers who constituted the original Kosciuszko Squadron are shown here on their way to Warsaw disguised as supply guards for the Red Cross. From left to right are Edward Corsi, George Crawford, Kenneth Shrewsbury, Carl Clark, Arthur Kelly, Merian Cooper and Edwin Noble.

Austrian-built Albatros D.III fighter planes of the Kosciuszko Squadron await their American pilots at an airfield in Poland. The stars and stripes on the squadron emblem symbolize Thaddeus Kosciuszko's contribution to the American Revolution.

where Bolshevik agitators launched a reign of terror to weaken the head of state, Marshal Józef Pilsudski.

Among the many foreign observers who were repelled by the acts of terrorism was a young American flying ace with a special family tradition of sympathy for Poland, Captain Merian C. Cooper. Born in Jacksonville, Florida, Cooper was a direct descendant of Colonel John Cooper, who had learned swordsmanship during the American Revolution from the Polish volunteer Colonel Casimir Pulaski. Young Merian Cooper had flown D.H.4s during World War I, was shot down and spent the summer and fall of 1918 in a German prison camp.

After the Armistice, Cooper was assigned to work in Poland for the American Relief Administration, which was providing medicines and food to areas ravaged by the War. Dismayed by Bolshevik atrocities, and believing that Poland would soon have to fight for its life against the Soviet Union, Cooper met with Marshal Pilsudski and offered to resign from the United States Army and organize a squadron of American pilots to fly for Poland. They would be called the Kosciuszko Squadron, after the Polish patriot Thaddeus Kosciuszko, who had fought in the American Revolution and then led an army in his own country's resistance to Russia in the 18th Century.

Encouraged by Marshal Pilsudski, Cooper went to Paris to formally receive his discharge from the American Army. A short time later he met with an old acquaintance, Major Cedric Fauntleroy, a Texan who had served in the French Foreign Legion before transferring to the famed 94th "Hat-in-the-Ring" Squadron when the United States entered World War I. Cooper recruited the recently discharged Fauntleroy to lead the new squadron, and six other demobilized American pilots

soon joined them: Captain Arthur Kelly and Lieutenants George Crawford, Edwin "Ig" Noble and Kenneth Shrewsbury, all of the Army Air Service; Lieutenant Carl Clark from the French Foreign Legion; and Captain Edward Corsi from the French Aviation Service. They traveled incognito to Warsaw as Red Cross guards on a supply train, arriving in September 1919.

Marshal Pilsudski, an old cavalry war horse, was not wholly convinced that an air force would have much effect on events to come, so he put the young mercenaries to work flying messages. In February 1920, the Bolsheviks launched their offensive against Poland, and in April the Marshal decided to counter with a thrust of his own into the Ukraine, where nationalists were struggling to end Russian domination. The Kosciuszko Squadron was moved to the Polish-Ukrainian border, where the Americans reconnoitered enemy troop movements. In early April, the Polish command supplied new Italian Ansaldo Balilla fighters to replace the squadron's aging Austrian-built Albatros D.IIIs.

The new planes arrived just in time. On April 25, 1920, the Polish Army attacked all along the front and Fauntleroy led the Kosciuszko Squadron against Bolshevik troops, cavalry and supply trains, using machine guns and light bombs. The Russian air force outnumbered the Polish Air Force, Kosciuszko Squadron included, but Russian pilots at first confined themselves to noncombat roles, withdrawing at the sight of enemy planes. Then a stroke of luck gave the Polish and American pilots total air superiority.

Merian Cooper was flying a routine mission when he sighted a large

Two of the Kosciuszko Squadron's new Balilla fighters lie in ruins at Luck, Poland, in May of 1920. Unaccustomed to his new Italian-made craft, the American pilot landed on top of his squadron leader's parked plane, damaging both aircraft beyond repair.

Following a second freak accident, the nose of a wrecked Austrian-built Albatros fighter assigned to the Kosciuszko Squadron pokes from a boxcar that it smashed into during a landing approach. The plywood plane was destroyed, but the pilot survived the crash.

white tent that looked like a cavalry headquarters. He and his wingman, Ig Noble, swooped down on the tent and riddled it with machine-gun fire. The Ukrainians reported later that the tent had been occupied by advance units of the Soviet air force. Utterly demoralized by the unexpected air attack, the Bolshevik pilots rushed back to Kiev, 400 miles to the rear. Cooper and Noble had unwittingly defeated them before they even got off the ground.

Railways were of vital importance to troop and artillery movements in the vast Ukraine, and the Kosciuszko Squadron specialized in harrying the rail lines and yards. Then, while diving at a racing locomotive, Noble was hit in the right elbow by antiaircraft fire. The wound crippled his arm, and he returned to the United States. But when word came that his last attack had enabled Polish prisoners on the train to escape into the forest, Noble was awarded Poland's highest medal for valor, the Virtuti Militari.

On another patrol, squadron commander Fauntleroy, while flying over a line of track through the forest, saw a large Bolshevik cavalry unit mining the rails and setting up an ambush. Around the next bend, Fauntleroy discovered why: A Polish troop train was steaming toward the trap. He dived and waved frantically until someone on board pulled the brake; then he landed in a clearing, dashed to the locomotive and warned the train crew of the ambush ahead. Polish soldiers quickly poured from the train and picked their way through the woods to devastate the Soviet troops from the rear. Marshal Pilsudski later gave Fauntleroy as well the Virtuti Militari.

Stunning advances brought the Polish forces deep into the Ukraine. On May 7, they captured the key city of Kiev, and the Kosciuszko Squadron moved to a new base at nearby Beluga Tserkov to enjoy a brief respite while the Soviets regrouped. The pilots would need their rest. Annoyed by the performance of the Red Army, Soviet leaders rallied the troops and poured in reinforcements. The resurgent Red Army counterattacked, forcing the overextended Poles back from Kiev.

The Polish Air Force and the Kosciuszko Squadron were thrown in to help block the Russian onslaught. Flying around the clock, the American pilots pinpointed Soviet vanguard units, dropped messages to warn nearby Polish commanders and then attacked the advancing Soviets with bombs and machine guns. It was probably the first time that aviation had been employed as a rear guard for an army in full retreat, and the American volunteers developed tactics against both trains and cavalry that bogged the Soviet Army down for days. Each time they encountered a train, the pilots strafed the locomotive to disable it and scatter the guards, enabling Polish ground units to capture some trains virtually unopposed.

Coming upon a column of Soviet cavalry, a pilot would approach at treetop level, drop bombs on the wagons, and then rake the men and

In Warsaw, Polish leader Marshal Józef Pilsudski (second from right) decorates five members of the Kosciuszko Squadron with the Cross of Valor on the day before their demobilization in 1921.

their mounts with machine guns. With the engine roaring its loudest to terrorize the horses, the flier would tip the nose of his fighter up and down as he zoomed over the heads of the horsemen, spraying bullets along the entire length of the column. The cavalrymen's only recourse was to dismount and hold their screaming horses by the reins, while trying to get in a few shots at the passing aircraft.

So successful were Cedric Fauntleroy's pilots and tactics that Marshal Pilsudski assigned him to overall command of four squadrons—three from the Polish Air Force, plus the Kosciuszko Squadron—and promoted him to lieutenant colonel. At the same time, Merian Cooper was promoted to major and given command of the American mercenaries. But his command would be short-lived: On July 13 he mysteriously disappeared while on a flight over enemy territory.

With its numbers rapidly diminishing, the Kosciuszko Squadron looked for fresh volunteers from the United States. Twenty-three pilots enrolled, but the Department of State blocked their passports: Despite sympathy for the Polish cause, Washington was apprehensive that the American people would not approve of even an implied involvement in a new European conflict. Besides, a Soviet victory over Poland seemed imminent, and there was no point in permitting American mercenaries to serve in a lost cause.

And then, with a Russian army pressing at the outskirts of Warsaw, the tide of battle suddenly turned. Marshal Pilsudski rallied his air and ground forces and launched a series of stunning counterattacks that forced the enemy to retreat from Polish soil. An armistice was declared on October 18, 1920.

Nearly seven months later, the mysterious disappearance of Merian Cooper was explained. Shot down by machine-gun fire, Cooper had crashed into the midst of a Cossack cavalry formation. The whooping horsemen rode in tight circles around Cooper's plane as he climbed out of the wreckage, and the Cossack commander ordered his men to strip and search the pilot. Cooper, who carried no identification, was left standing in a pair of U.S. Army surplus undershorts with "Cpl. Frank Mosher" stenciled across them. A scheme sprang into Cooper's mind. His name was well known to the Soviets and would surely bring him execution or brutal treatment. But as the unknown Corporal Mosher, he might be able to pass himself off as a hapless American who had been forced to fight against the Bolsheviks. It was worth a try — and it succeeded: His captors accepted him as Mosher, an unwilling combatant in the conflict between Poland and the Soviet Union. But they hardly treated him as an honored guest. Thrown into a prisoner-of-war camp deep inside Russia, he nearly died from typhus. After nursing himself back to health, Cooper joined two Polish fellow prisoners in escaping and made his way back to Poland to rejoin the Kosciuszko Squadron on May 10, 1921 — the day before the squadron was disbanded. Twelve years later, Cooper was to achieve success in a very different endeavor — as coproducer of the classic Hollywood film *King Kong*. ➤➤

2
To Spain for glory, money and a cause

Half of Madrid seemed to be on the rooftops, at the windows or in the streets, cheering itself hoarse as the squadron of stubby Soviet-built Polikarpov I.15 biplanes roared across the battered masonry canyons between the taller buildings. It was April 9, 1937, and after months of fighting, the Spanish Republican forces still clung to Spain's historic capital as the rebel Nationalist army of General Francisco Franco—backed by Germany and Italy—laid siege to the city from three sides. Now, bolstered by Soviet fighter aircraft, Soviet combat pilots and a handful of international mercenary volunteers, the Republican air arm was appearing in force—for the first time in months—to bomb and strafe the rebel positions in the Casa de Campo, across the Manzanares River from Madrid. As the Polikarpovs finished a pass over the enemy and swooped above the city in preparation for another attack, the rooftop audiences screamed their approval.

The noisy little biplanes were painted Soviet forest green and pale blue gray, with red Republican bands on the wings and fuselage. One particularly aggressive plane, marked with the white numerals "56," was being flown as usual by an American going under the name of Francisco Gomez Trejo. His real name was Frank Tinker, and he was the best freelance pilot in the Spanish Civil War. He was amazed at the onlookers' enthusiasm: "As we roared past the taller buildings," he wrote later, "we could see them jumping up and down and waving everything they could lay their hands on. Of course, we couldn't hear the cheering—our planes were making too much noise—but we could almost feel the waves of acclamation emanating from them."

For soldiers of fortune like Frank Tinker, the applause was particularly welcome—and symbolic. For more than a decade, ever since the reverberations of World War I had quieted across Europe and the upheaval in the Soviet Union had grown still, mercenary pilots had been out of work, scrounging for odd jobs through the hobo jungles of aviation. Now they had found an arena again: Spain. Here they could test their skills and nerve, seek the thrills on which they thrived, fatten their

Wheeling in the sky above Madrid, Republican fighter aircraft defend the city against attacks by Nationalist bombers during the early months of the Spanish Civil War. Mercenary pilots from many countries flew for the Republican side in this epochal conflict.

wallets, serve the cause of right, raise hell with their comrades, tell stories, fly fast planes and shoot down others. The Spanish Civil War provided not only an arena but an audience—and not just of Spaniards on rooftops. The whole world watched, spellbound by the heroism and the horror. A flying soldier of fortune could win international recognition here, fame, perhaps even immortality. For many mercenaries, this new war was positively welcome after their years of inaction.

After Europe had settled into peace after World War I, unemployed fliers had drifted homeward with faraway looks in their eyes and only a few foreign coins to jingle in their pockets. In America a surfeit of pilots—some of them demobilized Army aviators, others longtime mercenaries fresh out of work—was loosed upon their countrymen, to learn to walk if they could. For those who could not fall in step on the ground, flying shows and barnstorming were ways to stay aloft. But for some aviators even the undeniable thrills of stunt flying and wingwalking, or of parachuting over the crowds, were not enough.

Men like Floyd Hurtial "Slats" Rodgers found money and danger in bootlegging, the closest thing to a shooting war that a footloose pilot could find during much of the late 1920s and early '30s—unless he wanted to fly for the wily warlords of China. From Paris, Charles Kerwood, who had cut his teeth on combat over the trenches, made his way to the Balkans, where Greece and Turkey were at war once again. Kerwood flew briefly for Greece in 1922, then drifted back to Paris. There he learned that the French were putting down an uprising in North Africa; he offered to organize an American volunteer squadron for the Moroccan front and was soon machine-gunning Berber horsemen in the dunes.

Dean Ivan Lamb, who had emptied his gun at Phil Rader in the inconsequential dogfight over the Mexican desert in 1913, headed for Central America. During the years since he had flown for Pancho Villa, Lamb had been a pilot with Britain's Royal Flying Corps, and he claimed to have shot down one of the first German Gotha bombers to fall on English soil. After the Armistice, he kept himself aloft flying mail on the New York-Chicago run before moving to Latin America to earn his keep as an air courier. He attracted brief attention in 1921 when he was said to have made the first flight between the Honduran cities of San Pedro Sula and Tegucigalpa, over an 11,000-foot mountain range.

According to Lamb's own account of his adventures, which is larded with exaggerations, he then wandered south to Buenos Aires, where he fell in with a wild bunch of out-of-work European combat pilots and was approached by both sides of the Paraguayan civil war and asked to lead their rude air forces. Lamb claimed that he chose the side with the most planes and "gave" the other air force to his friend, an Italian pilot named Mazzolini. Lamb bragged that he and the other pilots could stage fake air duels so convincingly that it was unnecessary to do more than mock battle for the benefit of their respective employers. The lesson Lamb had learned in his noisy but harmless Mexican dog-

The Black Eagle's flights of fancy

Hubert Fauntleroy Julian, who liked to style himself the "Black Eagle," was the very embodiment of the bravado that characterized so many aerial soldiers of fortune. During his long career the dapper Julian, one of the first black aviators, was a stunt parachutist, mercenary pilot and international arms dealer. But he was perhaps best known for his brief service as commander of Ethiopian Emperor Haile Selassie's air force.

Invited to perform aerial stunts and parachute jumps at the African leader's coronation ceremonies in 1930, Julian so impressed his host during a preliminary exhibition that he was rewarded with Ethiopian citizenship, the rank of colonel and command of the Emperor's fledgling three-plane air force. The gem of this trio, a de Havilland Gypsy Moth, was Selassie's personal plane, and the monarch had ordered that the craft was not to be flown until his coronation.

Heedless of the Emperor's orders and intent on impressing the crowds who gathered to see a rehearsal two days before the ceremony, the Black Eagle surreptitiously took the prized Moth aloft, roared into full view of the assembled multitudes and performed a number of aerial maneuvers. Descending for a low-altitude pass, he tugged gently on the stick to level off, but the untested Moth did not respond.

Julian's reward for the resulting crash was a one-way ticket home. Upon arriving in New York, the irrepressible Black Eagle dismissed all criticisms of his Ethiopian venture. "I can state categorically," he told reporters, "that the Emperor and I were the best of pals when I left."

The dapper Colonel Julian emanates aplomb on his return to New York from Ethiopia in 1930. The former chief of the Ethiopian air force blamed his dismissal on envious subordinates, charging that they "even tried to poison me after tampering with every plane I took up."

Julian trains recruits after returning to Ethiopia in 1935. He had hoped to fly against the invading Italians, but the Emperor grounded him.

fight with Rader was at last being put to regular professional use.

Such deceits could perhaps be forgiven in light of the economic depression that swept the world in the 1930s and made it even harder for pilots to find work. But what could not be overcome was the boredom that soon became chronic. Bush wars and petty revolutions provided only temporary employment and no job security. Mercenary fliers were always on the move, returning from one country, departing for another, boasting loudly to cover the silence. Some tried speed racing, attempted record distance flights or piloted the aircraft of polar explorers. Between odd jobs they always seemed to be waiting for something to happen, which never did. Real life was not far removed from the staccato portraits in Hollywood films of the 1930s—an image of the uneasy ex-combat pilot forever frozen along with that of the down-and-out cowboy.

For the hard-core soldiers of fortune, especially the disappointed romantics and those to whom passion for a cause was an essential part of flying, something was needed. In 1936 they got their wish at last in Spain, where Right-Wing Nationalist rebels led by Francisco Franco were waging a civil war to overthrow the duly elected Left-Wing Republican government (whose adherents were called Loyalists). There, in a new kind of cold-blooded, deadly air warfare over the snow-swept mountain peaks of the Guadarrama range north of Madrid, above the gnarled hills of the Basque country, and over the dusty brown valleys of Andalusia, mercenary pilots fought and died violently on the eve of World War II. By the time the Spanish Civil War was over, even the most naïve idealist who had rushed to fight for Spain in the International Brigades was aware that it had been only a cruel prelude, and that something great and tragic was about to befall the earth.

Passion alone set the pilots in Spain apart from the maverick aviators who had flown the world's backwaters over the previous decade. Many of those who flew for the Republicans saw the War as a desperate fight to save Spain from a tyrannical Fascist upstart whose rebellion might have failed without the decisive backing of Adolf Hitler and Benito Mussolini. The very few freelance fliers who joined the Italian and German aviators in flying for the Nationalist cause believed that they were striking an urgent blow against Communist Russia, which was coming to the aid of the Republicans.

The fact that the United States declared itself neutral, and refused to sell military supplies either to the Spanish government or to Franco, deeply offended some of the American mercenary pilots flying for the Republicans. Two of them, Derek Dickinson and Eugene Finick, wrote an impassioned appeal to Secretary of State Cordell Hull:

"We, as Pilots and loyal American Citizens (in the Past), earnestly urge the Government of the United States of America to discontinue the measures that have prevented aid and assistance to the legitimate Government of Spain, elected by the Majority of the Spanish People." The letter, conveyed to Washington through the United States air attaché in

Valencia, Captain Townsend Griffiss, argued that Spain needed American help "to resist the mercenary rule of the Fascists under Franco." Echoing the apprehensions of many Europeans and Americans at the time, the pilots argued: "We are not fighting for War, but to prevent another catastrophe equal to the 1914 European conflict."

The Iberian Peninsula had indeed become a trial ground for some greater war, particularly for a future air war. Military observers in Germany, Italy, England, France and the United States were watching closely, evaluating the merits of machine guns, bombing systems, fighter and bomber deployment, formation tactics and the relative merits of speed versus maneuverability in new aircraft being tested over Spain.

Whole squadrons of foreign fliers were sent off to get their first taste of combat in Spain. Hundreds of Italian aviators arrived with nimble Fiat fighters to support thousands of Italian ground troops sent to assure Franco's success. From Germany came swarms of Luftwaffe pilots, and soon the Spanish skies were the domain of Hitler's Condor Legion, equipped with Heinkel and Messerschmitt fighters and the deadly Stuka dive bomber. Ranked against them were the Soviets with their Polikarpov I.15 biplane, called the *Chato,* or snub nose in Spanish, and the hot Polikarpov I.16 monoplane, nicknamed the *Mosca,* or fly.

In addition to the German, Italian and Russian pilots sent to Spain by their governments were several groups of independent volunteers—one, the Escuadrilla España, formed by the French writer André Malraux *(pages 47-49).*

Other freelance pilots arrived individually, among them Britons, Yugoslavs, Dutchmen, Swiss, Frenchmen, Czechs and Americans. Usually they were given reconnaissance or bombing missions in any antiquated aircraft that was available, and they seldom stayed for more than a few months. The violence and carnage around them was grimmer than any of them could have expected.

One of the first groups of American adventurers on the scene discovered soon enough that there was more to Spain's agony than thrills and quick money. The best-known member of this hapless group was Bert Acosta, who had flown as pilot for Commander Richard E. Byrd on Byrd's transatlantic flight in 1927. With him came speed racer Edward Schneider, along with Gordon Berry and Major Frederick Lord, both of whom had flown for the British in World War I. They embarked from New York in November 1936 with a promise of $375 a week plus a bonus for each Nationalist plane shot down.

When they reached their air base, the four Americans found that they were to fly obsolete commercial aircraft fitted with bomb racks but no guns. Lord wrote later: "That hangar contained two English Miles sport jobs, a couple of Monospars with tiny Pobjoy motors, an old cabin Farman with a J-6 motor, a Vickers two-seater reconnaissance job with a prop that looked like a telephone pole, a J-6 Fokker tri-motor passenger plane, and two Breguet two-place bombers of 1925 vintage." Elsewhere the Republicans had old Nieuports and Loires, Potezes and a few

World War I de Havillands. Said pilot Eugene Finick: "We'd have taken planes out of the Smithsonian if we could have got them."

Each day, Acosta and his friends were to fly as far as 30 miles into enemy terrain, drop their bombs and return, protected whenever possible by an escort of *Chatos*. But they got off to a bad start when Lord tried to show their Spanish squadron leader how dangerous their aircraft really were. As Lord told it, he took his commander up in a Breguet biplane and had just reached 2,000 feet when the upper wing collapsed. The Spaniard signaled for Lord to climb higher so they could use their parachutes, but Lord refused—he had seen ground crewmen sleeping on the silk chutes on the wet floor of the hangar, and wet silk is not inclined to unfurl. Lord preferred to take his chances and try to land with the damaged wing. But as soon as the plane was on the ground, the enraged Spanish officer ordered Lord arrested; only the intervention of some burly Spanish mechanics rescued him from the firing squad.

The Americans provoked the Spaniards even more with their ground conduct, typified by a string of drunken brawls. And they behaved little better in the air. According to a United States Embassy intelligence report, Acosta had taken to flying with a brandy bottle in one hand and his cigarettes in the other. His pals, the report explained, insisted that he was such a brilliant, instinctive pilot that it was unnecessary for him to be conscious while on a mission.

So sour were relations by Christmas that Acosta and his cronies decided that it would be prudent to chuck the whole mess. They were flying at the time in the Basque countryside of northwestern Spain. France was just across the Bay of Biscay, so they hired a boat to smuggle them from Bilbao to Biarritz. But before they could weigh anchor the Spaniards got wind of their scheme, shot their boatman and hauled the four sheepish adventurers before the Air Ministry in Valencia. That unfortunate interview ended with Bert Acosta being thrown out of the Air Ministry bodily. The honeymoon was over. The wayward Americans were given papers permitting them to leave Spain and were hustled to the French border. From France they sailed on the liner *Paris* for home.

When they disembarked in New York, they told their story to an eager press. They were also questioned by federal authorities, who seized their passports and ordered them to appear before a grand jury that was investigating the procurement of Americans to fight in Spain. The State Department, seeking to emphasize America's neutrality, had dusted off a 1907 law that stripped the citizenship of any American who "has taken an oath of allegiance to any foreign state." Bert Acosta and company had carefully avoided taking any such oath, and they were freed. The State Department was also seeking to discourage Americans from joining either side in Spain by stamping all passports: "Not good for travel to Spain." This made it possible to impound the passports of those who went anyway, on the ground that the passports had been obtained under false pretenses. But taking away citizenship was an

André Malraux (left), commander of the Escuadrilla España, and Abel Guides, his eventual successor, stand beside one of the squadron's Potez bombers. Although unable to pilot a plane himself, Malraux flew 65 missions as a bombardier-gunner.

This poster advertises the 1938 film Espoir—titled in English Man's Hope—made by Malraux and based on the war experiences of his squadron. Malraux also wrote a novel about the Spanish Civil War with the same English title.

Commander Malraux's Bohemian air corps

After the uprising against Spanish democracy began in July 1936, one of the first foreigners to rally to the Republican cause was French author André Malraux. He raised money to buy French planes—mostly Potez 540 bombers—for the Republicans, who then authorized him to recruit a squadron of foreign mercenary pilots.

Malraux's Escuadrilla España became the hub of a bustling café society of journalists and camp followers who met at Madrid's Hotel Florida. According to a biographer, Malraux always "appeared fresh-shaven for evening cocktails, retelling crazy dogfight details and discussing the military and political situation." For all of its flair, the unit was not an effective fighting force. By December it had lost half its men and planes and it was later absorbed into the Republican air force.

LE
MOUVEMENT DE LIBÉRATION NATIONALE
présente
ESPOIR
SIERRA DE TERUEL
Un film d'ANDRÉ MALRAUX
Musique de DARIUS MILHAUD
Une Production CORNIGLION-MOLINIER
Réalisé en Espagne pendant la guerre civile

A Dewoitine 372 fighter gets ready to take off from France for Spain on the 6th of August, 1936. Two days later, France's Prime Minister, Léon Blum, signed a pact that outlawed all arms shipments across the border between France and Spain.

Members of Malraux's unit gather in front of a Potez 540 bomber, a cumbersome craft that was easy prey for enemy fighters.

Trailed by an enemy fighter, a smoking Dewoitine of the type flown by the Escuadrilla España plunges earthward after losing a dogfight.

federal officials who took an interest in his passport. In his thick Arkansas accent—he pronounced his own name "Tanker"—he claimed that he was the son of Spanish immigrants to Mexico who had entered the United States illegally and then died, leaving him an orphan to grow up among cotton pickers in Arkansas. Now, he explained, he was simply going home to the land of his birth. The officials were probably suspicious, but they let him go. Tinker ended up sailing alone, because the others, like Dahl, had made alternative travel arrangements.

Tinker and Dahl were part of a group of five highly trained American fighter pilots recruited at about the same time, the three others having enlisted in New York on the understanding that they could sign contracts in Spain after they proved they could handle fighter planes. They were James Allison of Texas, Charles Koch of New York and Albert J. Baumler of New Jersey. Tinker caught up with them at the Republican air base at Los Alcazares, where they underwent final testing in 1925 Breguets. Both Tinker and Dahl passed easily and were soon on their way with Allison and Koch to another airfield at Manises (Baumler also passed his tests but was given an assignment at Alicante). At Manises they were to fly with a group of British volunteers in single-engined Breguet bombers.

This Anglo-American squadron flew its first mission against a target near the city of Teruel, where the fighting was fierce. The mission was a fiasco. The pilots were instructed to strike the place that was bombed by the squadron ahead of them. But the vanguard squadron was harassed by Italian Fiats and never got around to dropping its bombs. Not knowing where to bomb, and with no way of communicating with the other squadron, Tinker's group turned back. On landing, one of the British aviators veered to avoid another plane and nosed over on the field. The pilot and his observer escaped serious injury, but their Breguet was destroyed.

The four Americans in this luckless squadron soon proved themselves as bomber pilots and won welcome transfers to a newly formed fighter unit. More welcome still was news that they would be flying the Soviet Chato biplane, one of the best fighter aircraft in Spain at the time. Their squadron leader would be the black-haired Captain Andrés García La Calle, who had worked his way up from sergeant and had distinguished himself as a fighter pilot in an outmoded Nieuport.

For the first few days, Tinker and his friends practiced formation flying, machine-gunned targets towed behind a Russian plane, and familiarized themselves with the Chatos. The fuselage and wings, Tinker discovered, had been manufactured in the Soviet Union, but the engines were Wright Cyclones made in New Jersey. Compared with the other planes he had flown so far in Spain, the Chato was a joy to fly. It handled almost like the swift and maneuverable Boeing F-4B that Tinker had flown for the United States Navy. He and Whitey Dahl and the others managed to impress their Spanish officers with their effortless command of the Chatos, and two weeks later they were sent to an

Three Republican Breguet XIX bombers blast a Nationalist bridge in a raid during the first months of the Spanish Civil War. These were the planes flown by American mercenary pilots Frank G. Tinker and Harold E. "Whitey" Dahl in early 1937.

Harold E. "Whitey" Dahl, seen here next to No. 54, his Polikarpov I.15 Chato, was considered an outstanding pilot by his squadron commander, Andrés García La Calle, who remarked that Dahl was "more aggressive" than his fellow American mercenary, Frank Tinker (opposite).

airfield near Guadalajara for combat duty—minus Charlie Koch, who could not adjust to Spanish food and was soon in the hospital.

"At Guadalajara we found ten sleek looking monoplane fighters," Tinker noted later, adding erroneously that the planes were "almost exact copies of our American Army fighters of the P-26 type." In fact, he had seen his first Soviet *Mosca,* whose retractable landing gear, streamlined design and powerful engine made it far superior to the P-26. But not everyone was allowed to pilot the *Moscas.* "Experienced Russian combat pilots were flying them," Tinker wrote. "If we were good boys throughout the war, we might be allowed to fly these ships after the Armistice was signed."

A large building at one corner of the field had been refurbished with carpeting and draperies from the palace of the local duke and was turned over to the foreign pilots. There the Americans and Russians got acquainted. "All were using Spanish names," Tinker recalled. "The Russian commander, Captain Ramón, was especially interested in us Americans. The Russians had been there a little more than two months, so their knowledge of Spanish was about as limited as ours. Both sides depended upon an interpreter. La Calle had told us how slim our chances were of ever flying those monoplanes, so we took no pains to get on the good side of the Russians."

The Americans themselves were now becoming a tight group—Tink-

er, Dahl, Allison and Ben Leider, a New York newspaperman who was a member of the Communist Party and had come to Spain with no military flying experience to fight for the cause.

"Ben was the serious-minded one," Tinker said, adding that Leider "would sometimes give us very comprehensive talks on world politics. I wasn't a member of any party, but I would frequently get into arguments with Ben over the social system down South. He was much admired by the rest of us for the fact that, with no previous military training, he had volunteered for duty in fighter planes."

Whitey Dahl, with his shock of blond hair and his ruddy features, was the one who really stood out. He had housed Edith at a hotel in Valencia, but she found that wartime life in the city left something to be desired. Whitey had at last agreed to let her move up the Mediterranean coast to the French Riviera at Cannes, where she could make better use of her long hours away from him—with the help of his hefty salary and the bonuses he hoped would soon be rolling in. "Dahl wrote to her incessantly. His infatuation with his wife," Tinker observed, "was a constant source of wonder to the Spaniards."

After settling themselves in at Guadalajara, the members of the American Patrol, as the group was called, began the serious work of air war. Their first missions were to bomb two enemy gunpowder factories on the Jarama River. They flew nine planes, with García

La Calle's in the lead and the others trailing to form a large V formation made up of three smaller Vs. The Soviet pilots came up in three monoplanes to watch the new arrivals in flight. Tinker watched them back, marveling again at how wicked the streamlined *Moscas* looked in the air. "With their wheels up," he wrote later, "they were very little more than a wing, a motor, and two machine guns." He resolved to do his best to get to fly one.

On one of these first missions of the squadron, the Communist newspaperman Ben Leider scored the Americans' first victory—without firing a shot. Leider got on the tail of a German Heinkel 51 fighter but for some reason did not use his machine guns. The German pilot, seeking to escape his pursuer, dodged down to treetop level and, with Leider still behind him, brushed a tree, lost control of his plane and crashed to the ground. Soviet monoplanes had brought down four additional He 51s, so there was a joint celebration at the local hotel that night.

Charged with enthusiasm, the squadron went up a few days later, on February 18, only to tangle with a swarm of two-dozen He 51s. Faced with odds of close to 3 to 1, the pilots obediently followed García La Calle into the circular defensive formation that he had specified for unfortunate moments like this. In response, the Heinkels veered off and dived below, where some of them flew around lazily. It was too much for Ben Leider, who started down after one of the easy-looking targets and was instantly pounced upon by three other waiting German fighters. Tinker saw Leider's plane give a twitch, then wander off in a shallow dive before crashing into a hill. Leider was the first American volunteer to die in Spain.

Allison and Dahl also took the bait. Allison managed to shoot down his quarry before the other Heinkels could get on his tail; then his plane was hit, but he managed to wheel about and head for home. Dahl was not so lucky. He was unable to shoot his target before three Heinkels were upon him, shooting off his entire tail section. From his lofty vantage point, Tinker saw a white parachute blossoming but could not tell whose it was.

By then, Tinker had problems of his own. After taking up his spot in the circle, he had looked up and seen an enemy plane heading toward him. At first, he said later, he "merely glanced at it and noted that it made a rather pretty sight with the sun showing through a haze behind it. Then I glanced back again and noticed that there were little flashes coming through his propeller blades. He was shooting at me."

Tinker swung around into a sharp left banking dive, came out behind and beneath his attacker, fired for a few seconds, then rejoined the circling formation. Twice again he was attacked the same way, and then the deadly Soviet *Moscas* came to the rescue and the balance shifted. The *Moscas* took on the Heinkels lurking above, while Tinker's squadron fell upon the enemy below. Within 15 minutes they were in control, and seven He 51s had gone down. But it was a sad return to their base: Tinker was the only American to reach home.

Allison had been seen heading for home, but he had not arrived. Dahl and Leider were down—and Leider was certainly dead.

Gloom decended on the field, but that did not prevent García La Calle from a gruff lecture after first priming his pilots with beer. "Comrades, today our squadron lost three planes," he said. "It was entirely unnecessary. The pilots disregarded the instructions and warnings which had been given them." They had indeed been told of the importance of defensive formations; they had been warned of the Heinkels' superior diving speed; they had been reminded to think of other enemy planes besides the one at which they were firing. "The pilots who are missing," said García La Calle sternly, "forgot all three of these warnings. They left the formation, they knew there were Heinkels above, and they had eyes only for the planes at which they were firing." Then he discoursed on the tactics of modern air war and the glory of dying for the cause and passed out more beer.

That night the squadron received a phone call that lifted the pilots' spirits. Dahl was alive. He had parachuted among friendly forces, landing in an olive grove where local farmers loaned him a donkey to ride to the nearest military command post. He would rejoin the squadron the next day. Then came another call: Allison had landed at another Republican field, with a bullet in his leg, and had to be hospitalized.

Dahl returned just in time for a bloody new offensive. So far the air war had consisted largely of bombing raids and dogfights. Now it changed dramatically to brutal attacks on ground forces. By March 1937, the thousands of Italian soldiers dispatched to Spain by Mussolini were tipping the balance for General Franco on the ground. Supported by tanks, three mechanized columns of Italians began advancing down the main highway from Saragossa to Madrid, through heavy rain. After waiting for the sky to clear, Tinker's squadron took to the air. Finding an opening in the cloud layer, the pilots dropped down to 600 feet to bomb the Italian columns, machine guns blasting.

The rains had made a quagmire of the countryside. Trenches filled with water almost as soon as they were dug, and the troops were almost totally exposed to the aerial onslaught. "We could see the poor devils scurrying through the mud in all directions," Tinker recalled later.

The attackers pounded the Italians in raid after raid. On one mission, while watching the results of Soviet bombing, Tinker noticed "a huge truck whirling end over end through the air, a most impressive sight." The Italians became jammed at an intersection, unable to leave the roadbed because of deep mud in the fields on both sides.

By then the troops were completely demoralized, flinging away rifles and ammunition belts as they scurried for cover. And as they ran they bunched together, making tempting targets for the pilots swooping above them. Tinker spotted one large group of soldiers in wild retreat and whipped down to attack them from in front. From about 700 feet he opened fire. Some of the Italians turned to run in the opposite direction, others struck out frantically to the sides. But it was too late.

"Already," Tinker later observed laconically, "they were falling like grain before a reaper." He continued his attack, spraying his bullets over a wider and wider area, until both fuel and ammunition ran low and he had to return to his base.

This brutal air assault disrupted the Italian thrust so thoroughly that Republican forces were able to consolidate their positions along the highway and block further advance. The squadron then returned to its previous routine of air-to-air combat, with Captain García La Calle leading the first patrol, Whitey Dahl the second and Frank Tinker the third. In a pitched battle with Italian Fiats, Tinker got behind one, fired a long burst and brought down his first enemy plane.

His next quarry was more elusive and slipped away before Tinker's bullets could find their mark. But Tinker still had other enemies to face: His squadronmates had drifted off, and as he looked above him he saw five Fiats ready to pounce. Tinker knew that the enemy planes could easily overtake him if he tried to reach the safety of a low-lying cloud bank far below him, so he decided to try a trick that he had learned at Army flight school. Dropping toward the clouds, he kept his eye on his rear-view mirror, framing the first of the pursuing Fiats. Then, just before

Preparing for takeoff, a Republican air force pilot revs up the engine of his Polikarpov I.16 Mosca, one of the finest fighter aircraft in Spain. Frank Tinker was overjoyed when he was permitted to fly this fast Soviet-built monoplane in combat.

the enemy pilot lined up on his plane, Tinker pulled into a sharp bank to the left. The Fiat, going too fast to follow, continued its screaming dive, while Tinker put his *Chato* through a 360-degree turn that put him directly behind the startled enemy airman. Tinker fired steadily until the next Fiat was lining up behind him, and then he executed the same maneuver again. He had done little or no damage to either plane but had succeeded in driving the attackers away. Tinker said that he used the identical trick on two more of the pursuing Fiats before finally gaining what he called "the comforting security of the clouds" and returning unharmed to a Republican base.

As time passed the number of the American mercenaries dwindled. One volunteer, Orrin Dwight Bell, had failed his flight test and had returned home. Derek Dickinson, the pilot who with Eugene Finick had written to the Secretary of State, had flunked the fighter check-out but had succeeded in an observation plane, so he was able to get a minor assignment in Barcelona. (Later, Dickinson would assert, in typical mercenary fashion, that he had challenged Bruno Mussolini to an air duel over the Mediterranean and had won on points, causing the Italian dictator's son to go home in disgrace.)

Jim Allison was returning to the United States because of his wounded leg. Charlie Koch had already left with his bad stomach, and soon Whitey Dahl was complaining of stomach trouble as well. Dahl was sent to Madrid for treatment and then managed to wangle permission to travel to Paris for an operation.

Frank Tinker, meanwhile, was making a name for himself. By attrition and by the sheer professional skill that he had demonstrated on the Guadalajara front and on his missions over Madrid, Tinker had become the top foreign freelance pilot in Spain. When García La Calle was promoted and given three squadrons to oversee, his replacement as squadron leader was so short on aerial combat skills that his men soon persuaded him to let Tinker command the unit in the air. Then another reward came Tinker's way from the Air Ministry: He was to be given the long-awaited chance to fly the Soviet *Mosca*. He would be flying with Soviet pilots and crack Soviet ground support. Joining him in this coveted assignment to a Russian squadron would be Al Baumler, the only other American pilot flying fighters at the moment, now that Whitey Dahl was on sick leave.

Baumler, who had been sent to a squadron at Alicante after his arrival in Spain, had done well for himself; he would eventually rack up a total of five confirmed kills. Like Dahl and Tinker, Baumler had been trained as an American military aviator, but a foolish accident—he had made a forced landing after neglecting to switch on a fuel tank in the twin-engined bomber he was flying—had kept him from completing advanced training at Kelly Field in San Antonio. He had tried to join United Air Lines as a copilot but then enlisted for Spain before he was hired. Together, Baumler and Tinker made their way to Alcalá de Henares to get acquainted with their Russian squadronmates.

They made their first flights in the hot *Mosca* monoplanes on May 30, 1937. "They were wonderful," Tinker wrote, noting that even the well-used training plane that he flew on his first flight "would make 250 miles an hour on the straightaway. What they would make in a dive I never found out—their airspeed meters did not go up that high." But he found that the planes had to be handled carefully. Twice, when he tried to use his usual biplane flying techniques, the *Mosca* went into a spin.

After a few missions flying their *Moscas* as escorts for squadrons of bombers, Tinker and Baumler and the Russians tangled with about 50 Nationalist fighters. After firing on seven or eight enemy planes Tinker finally managed to bring down one Fiat by setting its engine ablaze; he then—unintentionally, he said—shot the enemy pilot as he was preparing to parachute from his stricken craft. Tinker damaged his plane's left wing when landing after this engagement, and Baumler touched down with problems of his own: He had been hit in the back by shrapnel from explosive bullets fired at his tail section by an attacking Heinkel. Luckily the fragments had first passed through his steel seat back, so the wounds were superficial and he was soon back in action.

Three weeks later, Tinker was wounded far more gravely in his dignity. Left to his own devices one night in an Alicante villa maintained for foreign pilots on leave, he whiled away the time sampling bottles in the liquor cabinet. A stone jug marked *ginebra*—gin—convinced him that he owed it to himself to hit a nightspot in Valencia, 150 miles away. With incredible optimism, he bought an old bicycle from a shop down the street for the trip. By midnight, helped along by the gin, he had pedaled 15 miles and began to gather speed down a long, steep incline. Tinker's experience with bicycles had been mainly on American machines that were braked by pushing the pedals backward; this one had European-style handle-bar grip brakes. When he suddenly saw a pair of guards on the road Tinker started backpedaling furiously, but the bicycle kept speeding along. "I ran over one of the guards," he explained later, "and the other one promptly shot me down off my bicycle."

Luckily, it was a small-caliber bullet, and it missed Tinker's vital parts when it went through the right side of his abdomen. The guards tendered abject apologies when they discovered that they had shot a pilot from one of their renowned Soviet fighter squadrons, and Tinker was taken to a military hospital in Alicante. By July 12—a week after the start of the Battle of Brunete—he was back on duty and ready for three dogfights in as many flights. During his third engagement, he noticed a Soviet *Chato* being attacked by three new German Messerschmitt 109s. He led his two Russian wingmen to the rescue but arrived too late: The *Chato* was already on fire and going down out of control. Tinker shot down one of the attacking Messerschmitts while his two wingmen got one of the others. The third escaped. Back at the base, Tinker learned that the pilot of the doomed biplane had been Whitey Dahl, fresh back from a posthospital visit to the Riviera.

Baumler was gone next, with a swollen throat that required treatment

Albert J. Baumler, seen here in a Republican air force flight suit, was credited with five kills in aerial combat. Shortly before signing on to fly for the Spanish Republic, the 22-year-old Baumler had been dismissed as a United States Army Air Corps cadet for "failure to show proper flying proficiency."

in Valencia. When he was healthy again, Baumler went home, and Tinker found himself alone among strangers. One by one the Russians he had known had been rotated back to the Soviet Union, replaced by fresh Soviet pilots eager for combat experience. Given the language problems, Tinker could find only a few people to talk to. It was near the end of July 1937. The Spanish pilots in training in the Soviet Union were now returning to take over duties for the Republicans, and there was no longer a pressing need for foreign volunteers.

Tinker had now been in Spain for nearly seven months. He had scored eight confirmed kills, bringing him a total of $8,000 in bonuses over and above his salary. And he had accomplished his goal of flying the *Moscas.* He had had enough, and he sat down and wrote a letter to the Air Ministry terminating his contract. That same night he heard welcome news. Whitey Dahl had managed to bail out of his stricken plane and had landed unhurt in enemy territory. He had been taken prisoner and was in jail in Salamanca.

Dahl had had some frightening adventures. After scrambling out of his flaming *Chato's* cockpit and leaping into the air at 5,000 feet, he had drifted away from the scene of battle, his billowing parachute unseen by his squadronmates. Unfortunately, he had touched down amid a company of Franco's Moorish troops from North Africa. The Moors had been attacked from the air for days on end, and when they got their hands on Dahl they roughed him up and would have shot him if some Spanish officers had not arrived.

But Dahl knew that he was not yet out of danger. Jailed in Salamanca, he was visited by an Associated Press reporter who found the young pilot "running nervous fingers through his thinning blond hair" and pondering the prospect of a firing squad. It was not an idle fear: On October 5, 1937, he was taken from his cell, tried by a military court and sentenced to be shot.

The harsh sentence came as a shock to Edith Dahl, who had remained in France rather than risk trying to visit the imprisoned Whitey in war-torn Spain. Then she had a brain storm that made her devotion to Whitey into a news story that spread throughout the world. She wrote a letter to General Franco himself, pleading for the American pilot's life.

Her husband, she explained, was politically neutral and had signed up with the Republican air force only because he could not get a flying job in the United States. She then appealed to the Spanish leader's romantic sympathies, and to his vanity: "We have been married only eight months," she wrote. "I'm all alone. He flew only to get money for me. I know you are a man with a great heart and much courage. I give you my word that Harold will not fight you again if you have the compassion to give him his freedom and send him back to me. Now that victory is almost within your grasp, the life of one American pilot cannot mean much to you. I was an actress for several years but now I have found my happiness. Don't destroy it.

Please answer my letter so I may know what to do and if I can hope."

With her letter Edith enclosed a photograph that showed her in her best light—wearing a white bathing suit.

One week later she had her reply: a letter signed by the General and graced with the courtly, old-fashioned Spanish closure *"q.b.s.p."*—for *que besa sus pies,* (who kisses your feet). Edith's desperate try had worked; Dahl's life would be spared. (Only later did the Dahls learn that the strait-laced Franco had in fact seen neither the letter nor the picture. The communication had been intercepted by staff officers who, swayed either by Edith's sincerity or by her figure, had responded over the Spanish leader's signature.)

Whitey Dahl had been saved from execution, but he was not released from his Spanish captivity. "I'm going to be here a long, long time," he told a reporter who visited him in his cell. But Edith's stage career was given a boost by the publicity surrounding her famous letter, and she was soon appearing in French nightclubs, billed as "The Woman Who Melted Franco's Heart."

Edith was not the only American who was concerned about Dahl's welfare. Behind the scenes, the State Department made inquiries about the most famous American prisoner in Spain and was assured that he would probably be exchanged for a Nationalist captive held by the Republicans. Unfortunately, Whitey's poor sense of timing spoiled that likelihood. Unaware that he was to be traded, he wrote to Franco offering to fly for the Nationalist side free of charge rather than sit in his cell. Then he announced publicly: "I don't give a damn about a cause. I'm fighting for money." The Republicans swapped for someone else.

Dahl was held in Spain until February of 1940, nearly a year after the Civil War had ended with a Franco victory. Edith had recently gone back to the United States, where she was performing a Spanish dance routine on the vaudeville circuit, and she greeted Whitey somewhat coolly upon his return. He moved to Canada, where he became an instructor for the Royal Canadian Air Force. Edith joined him there for a time but then went back on the road as an entertainer, singing, dancing and playing the violin. Then Whitey married a Canadian woman, announcing that his Mexican nuptials with Edith had never been legal or binding. Edith, reached by reporters at a Salt Lake City theater—where she was appearing as "The Blonde Who Spiked the Guns of General Franco's Firing Squad"—was unperturbed. "I'm the best damned woman violinist in show business," she snapped, "and I don't need Dahl to sell a violin solo."

Frank Tinker, who had left Spain in August of 1937, also came home to problems. His passport seized by State Department officials when he stepped ashore in the United States, Tinker returned to Arkansas, where he brooded and attempted to find things to do. Spain was a hard act to follow. He wrote a book about his experiences, which was titled *Some Still Live.* He bought a canoe and paddled

Whitey Dahl's show-girl wife, Edith, who sent a photograph to Franco when pleading for her husband's life, smiles coyly in a revealing white dress. Hearing that Spanish officials who had seen her picture were eager to meet her, she said: "A smart girl ought to know when to stay home."

A rapidly aging Whitey Dahl sits alone and forlorn in the courtyard of a hospital in Salamanca, Spain. Dahl had been transferred from a Nationalist prison to the hospital, where he was granted a measure of freedom, but he had to be back in the hospital every night.

down the Mississippi to New Orleans with a pet fox terrier for company.

Seeking more excitement, he announced that he would get around the State Department's prohibition against his travel outside the country by flying a plane nonstop across the Atlantic to Spain. The State Department alerted the Civil Aeronautics Authority to stop him if he tried. He then wrote a letter to the War Department and the State Department applying for the job of air attaché in Spain. He was turned down curtly. During this period Al Baumler came to Tinker's hometown of De Witt for a brief nostalgic visit; he was back flying with the Army Air Corps and had suffered no consequences whatever for his service in Spain. He told Tinker that he was thinking of joining a new international outfit of mercenary pilots being organized to fight in China.

That sounded good to Tinker, but for the moment his heart was really set on Spain. Then the Republicans surrendered. A few weeks later, on June 13, 1939, after poring over his flight logs and Spanish maps, sitting alone in a Little Rock hotel room, Frank Tinker—also known as Francisco Gomez Trejo, and only 29 years old—picked up a .22-caliber pistol and shot himself in the chest. He left no message. ➤➤

Thrills and glamor in the funny papers

Inspired by the thrilling escapades of aerial soldiers of fortune, American cartoonists of the 1930s created comic-strip characters who rivaled—and in some cases surpassed—their real-life models for courage, romance and sheer seat-of-the-pants flying. In turn, these imaginary figures contributed to the myth of the mercenary by glamorizing a tawdry, deadly profession that in reality spawned as many rascals and ne'er-do-wells as it did heroes.

It is not surprising that comic strips featuring airborne

adventurers such as Captain Easy, Scorchy Smith and Smilin' Jack held millions of readers spellbound. During the joyless days of the Depression, comics were an inexpensive form of escapism. And in the vogue for aviation that followed Charles Lindbergh's epic flight across the Atlantic in 1927, comic-strip heroes who also happened to be pilots claimed a dedicated following all their own.

One such aviator was Captain Easy *(above)*, an unflappable American who becomes a spy for the Chinese air

GREAT! WHEN DO I START?

AT ONCE! BUT I WARN YOU, MY FRIEND, THE MISSION IS EXTREMELY DANGEROUS.

TWO THOUSAND MILES TO CHINESE TURKESTAN, ALMOST TO PERSIA EASY FLIES THE COUNTRY GROWS WILDER AND WILDER.

MORE THAN ONCE HE IS FIRED UPON

EASY, EAGER TO EXPLORE THIS STRANGE AND HOSTILE CITY AFOOT, FLIES OFF IN SEARCH OF A SAFE LANDING PLACE.

© 1933

THEN OVER SNOW-CLAD MOUNTAINS FOUR MILES HIGH, AS A SPY OF CHINA, INTO A LAND UNSEEN BY WHITE MEN SINCE THE DAYS OF MARCO POLO.

force in 1933, two years after China lost Manchuria to the Japanese. Instead of engaging in dogfights with Japanese pilots, however, Easy flies to the wholly mythical "lost province of Gungshi," a land unvisited by Europeans for seven centuries. Along the way, he is attacked by warriors who more closely resemble the 13th Century hordes of Genghis Khan than the Japanese fliers in modern warplanes who were to plague the real-life mercenaries who flew in China's defense.

How Scorchy scotched a corrupt revolution

Comics featuring mercenaries owed at least part of their widespread appeal to the enviable simplicity of the moral issues they espoused. No matter what war or rebellion was unfolding in the funnies, the hero always championed the right and winning side, and the villain worked for the side that would justifiably lose.

Scorchy Smith closely followed this rule. In one memorable episode, the clean-cut, virtuous Scorchy agrees to organize an air force for the government of Huaca, a fictitious South American country embroiled in revolution. Predict-

ably, the rebels' air force is led by a sleazy gangster named Knucks Maddox.

At first, Scorchy wants nothing to do with war—"It's all silly, useless and cruel," he says—and it is only when he learns that the rebels are out for personal profit, not the good of Huaca, that he decides to fight for the government. With right and wrong so clearly defined, it almost goes without saying that after many a cliff-hanger—like the aerial showdown pictured below—Scorchy finally defeats Knucks Maddox, the rebel fliers and all the other revolutionaries.

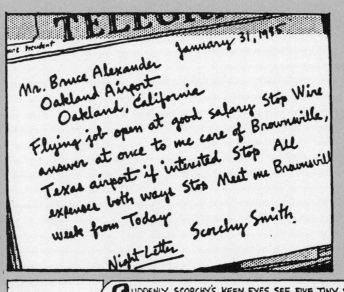

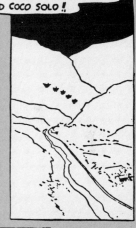

Smilin' Jack in a "wimmin" dilemma

No comic-strip pilot would seem quite complete without at least one curvaceous, adoring heroine at his side, but Smilin' Jack once lost his smile over two. In fact, for most of 1937 the hero of Zack Mosley's strip *Smilin' Jack* was torn between Bonita Caliente, the Latin American dancer he feels "honor bound" to marry for having saved his life, and stewardess Dixie Lee, the devoted sweetheart who is brokenhearted when Jack fails to propose *(below)*.

Of course, there was as much adventure as romance in Smilin' Jack's life. In a vain attempt to escape his problems with "wimmin," he took a job with a shabby Brazilian airline only to find himself flying with the Legion of Forgotten·Pilots, a gang of expatriate killers who performed aerial acrobatics to extort money from their terrified passengers.

After surviving the legionnaires' attempt to throw him from a plane, Jack soon put a stop to their racketeering, but he had to expend far more effort to escape the clutches of the persistent Bonita and convince Dixie of his love.

he would like to put it on every one of the P-40s in the group.

And so was born the lasting symbol of the world's most famous mercenary air force, a flamboyant, aggressive bunch of former United States Navy, Marine and Army pilots recruited quietly and slipped into Burma posing as missionaries, musicians and artists. Hired by China to guard the vital supply route known as the Burma Road, they flew in combat as a group for only seven months, from December 1941 to July 1942. But within days after Japan's December 7 attack on Pearl Harbor they were locked in aerial battle with fleets of Japanese warplanes and vaulted out of obscurity in the jungle to become perhaps the most famous American combat aviation unit of all time—the Flying Tigers. Under the unorthodox leadership of their maverick commander, Claire Lee "Old Leatherface" Chennault, this high-spirited group of curiously innocent American irregulars hardened quickly into an uncannily effective fighting force, destroying 297 enemy aircraft—and claiming 300 more—with a loss of only four American pilots killed in air combat.

Claire Lee Chennault was one of those superheated men on horseback whose courage, violent energies and unswerving opinions gain them a place in history as either madmen or geniuses. He was thoroughly detested by his adversaries, but he earned a passionate loyalty from his pilots. A born leader, he inspired his followers to attempt the impossible routinely and made them understand that he was prepared to bend or break every rule in the book on their behalf.

Born in Commerce, Texas, in 1890, Chennault was raised in the backwoods of northeastern Louisiana. As a youth he was encouraged to be self-reliant, and he grew to be combative, defiant, quick to take offense, determined to rank first—qualities abetted by the raw combustion of a quick mind. He entered Louisiana State University at the age of 14 and toyed with the notion of a military career until he visited the United States Naval Academy at Annapolis and saw the severe discipline and restrictions imposed on midshipmen. Preferring to follow his own path, he returned to Louisiana and found a teaching job. The income proved too meager to support his wife and the first of his eight children, so he switched from job to job to increase his earnings.

He was working as a laborer in an Ohio factory in April 1917 when America entered World War I. Chennault wanted to become an Army pilot, but at 26 he was thought too old for flight training. Commissioned in the infantry, he was soon stationed at Camp Travis in San Antonio, Texas, near Kelly Field, where he talked flight instructors into giving him lessons in their spare time. He won a nonflying assignment as supply officer of the 46th Aero Squadron, based at Roosevelt Field, Long Island, and looked forward to being sent overseas. But the War was drawing to a conclusion and he was disappointed to learn that no more air units were going to Europe. Instead, he was sent to help quell an uprising of angry black construction troops at Langley Field, Virginia.

When the deadly worldwide influenza epidemic of 1918 swept

through the ranks at Langley, Chennault was put in charge of a make-shift hospital ward. Then he himself was struck down by the disease, growing so weak that the medics stopped treating him and left him to die. Found by an officer he had known at Kelly Field, he was nursed back to health with the felicitous encouragement of bourbon whiskey, and by the time the War ended in November he was on his way back to Kelly, strong enough to accept assignment to flight school.

Once he had won his wings as a fighter pilot, he began demonstrating extraordinary skill in aerobatics. He also showed considerable flair as an aerial tactician. Fighter aces in the War had usually engaged in one-on-one jousting contests with enemy pilots; Chennault believed that three-plane combat formations would be much more effective, providing greater firepower, as well as team support and team defense. So he devoted himself to improving dogfighting tactics and adapting them to team flying, a cause that he promoted while teaching new pilots.

Chennault planted the germ of what would become another important innovation by sending men to the top of a water tower to watch for approaching "hostile" aircraft during war games. Using binoculars, the observers could see planes up to six miles away and warn their own pilots on the field below by loudspeaker. Later Chennault would expand and improve this primitive early-warning system by incorporating a network of telephones, radios and a central plotting office to work out the speed and direction of the enemy's approach. His system could give enough notice so that a squadron could be airborne before the enemy came into sight—a significant advance in the days before radar.

Chennault's radical ideas eventually got him into trouble with his Army Air Corps superiors, who believed that the development of swift and heavily armed bombers had made fighter aircraft ineffective in wartime. The bomber, they said, was invincible. Chennault disagreed and put his arguments to anyone within earshot. He also put them into a monograph that alienated many of his superior officers as soon as it was circulated. Among them was Lieutenant Colonel Henry H. "Hap" Arnold, who was to become commander of the American air arm. "Who is this damned fellow Chennault?" Arnold asked acidly.

The rejection by Air Corps brass embittered Chennault. It also ended his usefulness as an instructor of tactics, and in 1933 he was reassigned as the leader of a new Air Corps precision flying team. He and his wingmen—John Williamson and Haywood Hansell—called themselves "Three Men on a Flying Trapeze," from a popular ballad about the daring young man who swung through the air with the greatest of ease, and their team aerobatics made them famous at air shows across the country in the 1930s. When Hansell was transferred, he was replaced by William MacDonald, but when neither MacDonald nor Williamson was able to obtain a regular commission in the Air Corps, the two fliers decided to resign and look for civilian flying jobs.

The Flying Trapeze, forced to disband, gave its last performance in Miami early in 1936. In the audience was General Mao Pang-tso, of the

Chinese air force, who was impressed by the team's aerobatics. China badly needed men with such flying ability to defend itself against Japan, whose military forces had been pushing steadily south from Japanese-held Manchuria. And so far, most of China's efforts to enlist the help of foreign mercenary aviation advisers had met with failure—especially in the case of the irrepressible Weston Bert Hall.

After establishing himself as the rogue of the Lafayette Escadrille and then reputedly escaping by train across revolutionary Russia with the jewelry-laden wife of a czarist general, Bert Hall had all but vanished from public view. In 1921, he was divorced by his American wife, Bella May Byers—leaving her to raise Bert Jr. Hall's movements thereafter were frequently a mystery to all who knew him. To be sure, he surfaced now and again in Paris and Hollywood. And he managed to run up a growing roster of women who believed they were married to him: At ceremonies dedicating the postwar monument to the Lafayette Escadrille near Paris in 1928, three women claiming to be Mrs. Bert Hall showed up to occupy the same seat.

Then in 1929, the mythic Bert Hall was sprung on the world at large with the publication of his ghost-written memoirs, *One Man's War*. At the time, Hall himself seems to have been in China, where he had gone for the ostensible purpose of selling Douglas airplanes to the Chinese. In 1932, newspapers began publishing reports that Hall had become the head of the Chinese air force, and that he was known far and wide in China as the powerful General Chang Hui-chang. On April 27, 1930, even the *New York Times* announced to its readers that Hall had taken over China's air operations as a natural consequence of being the world's greatest flying adventurer.

"Scarcely a week goes by," the *Times* reported breathlessly, "without the appearance in the news of the name of some adventurer whose zest for excitement has led him into some remote corner to serve in some strange and dangerous capacity. Today it is Bert Hall, the American aviator." The paper went on to liken Hall to the already legendary Lawrence of Arabia and then to state: "The most outstanding aviator soldier of fortune is unquestionably this Bert Hall." The *Times* further related Hall's trumped-up story about flying for the Turks and then for their enemies the Bulgars in the Balkan War of 1912-1913, his stretch in the trenches with the French Foreign Legion, and his glory in the Lafayette Escadrille. Other newspapers also felt inspired to keep track of this famous aviator, and the Washington *Evening Star* would later tell its readers earnestly: "Over in China in the thick of the fighting is General Chang Hui-chang. He is commander-in-chief of the Chinese air forces, but his name isn't Chang at all, and he isn't even Chinese."

For that matter, Hall was not commander in chief either. In a grand exercise of self-glorification, he had created the role out of thin air—perhaps to publicize his book. On his arrival in politically divided China he had become an adviser to the chief of one faction's air force (whose name was General Chang Hui-chang). When Hall wrote to friends in America, he simply adopted the Chinese general's identity, claiming to be General Chang. After journalist Ernie Pyle discovered that there really was a living, breathing Chinese general of the same name, he wrote a story explaining that there were two generals involved, one named Chang, another called Chan who was actually Bert Hall, but that they commanded the air forces of opposing Chinese factions.

Hall had woven a tangled web. He was neither Chan nor Chang, and by June of 1931 he was in the process of swindling General Chang out of $100,000 in a deal to buy nonexistent Douglas bombers. Using a dummy corporation that he set up under the name of National Import Company, Hall got General Chang to place the $100,000 purchase price in escrow at the Canton branch of an American bank. Then Hall persuaded an unwary bank employee to transfer the funds to a San Francisco bank in the name of Floyd N. Shumaker, a pilot and crony of Hall's, who promptly went to the California bank and withdrew the $100,000. Meanwhile, Hall left China and headed for home.

Members of the United States Army precision flying team—from left, William MacDonald, Claire Chennault and John Williamson—relax in 1935 next to a Boeing P-12 pursuit plane at Maxwell Field, Alabama. Eventually, all three men became aviation advisers to Chinese leader Generalissimo Chiang Kai-shek.

Costly crashes illustrate the Chinese air force's need in the 1930s for the services of a skilled mercenary adviser like Claire Chennault. The Vultee dive bomber (left) and Hawk fighter (bottom center) were wrecked by ill-tutored Chinese pilots; the runway collision (top) and the upended Dewoitine D-510 fighter (right) were both the work of foreign instructors.

Suspecting that something was amiss, General Chang and an aide sped to the American consulate in Canton to recover the funds. The situation threatened to create an embarrassing diplomatic incident, and after diligent inquiries by the consulate and the American bank, Hall's California accomplice, Shumaker, was arrested but released on bond soon afterward. When Hall landed in California in late August he was clapped into the Los Angeles County Jail. He raised $25,000 bail for his release—and then, to everyone's surprise, the Chinese dropped the charges, possibly because General Chang stood to lose too much face if court proceedings revealed how thoroughly he had been duped.

Never one to quit while he was ahead, Hall returned to China, where in 1933 he was caught swindling another Chinese general, this time for a mere $10,000, in a deal for 1,000 nonexistent Mauser pistols and ammunition. After cajoling a Chinese bank into cashing the general's I O U, Hall slipped out of China on the steamer *Choko Maru,* bound for Kobe, Japan, where he planned to board a ship for America.

But Hall had failed to take into account the enterprising American consul general in Tientsin, F. P. Lockhart. Learning of the latest swindle, Lockhart persuaded his counterpart at the Japanese consulate to have Hall's voyage extended. When the *Choko Maru* docked in Kobe, Hall was not allowed to disembark but was obliged to sail back to China to face the music. Arrested and taken to Shanghai for trial by the United States Consular Court, he was convicted and sentenced to two and a half years at McNeil Island Federal Penitentiary in Washington State.

Bert Hall was shipped unceremoniously to prison in his native land. Apparently chastened by his incarceration, he settled thereafter with a new wife—a Hollywood dancer—in the placid township of Castalia, Ohio. There, during World War II, he and a partner would turn a simple shed into a factory producing flimsy balsawood models of the Germans' V-2 rocket for children to catapult out of slingshots. Hall called his enterprise the Sturdy Toy Company. He could not resist.

The end of the Chinese road for Bert Hall had hardly marked the end of China's own painful journey. At the mercy of inept or unscrupulous foreign advisers like Hall, the Chinese air force in the late 1930s remained a paper tiger. It was supposed to have a force of 500 airplanes, but there were only about 100 aircraft in China fit for combat. The air service was riddled with corruption, and after inadequate instruction by a training mission from Italy, the pilots were equipped with fancy diplomas and little else. In the face of mounting Japanese aggression, the powerful Chinese Nationalist leader, Generalissimo Chiang Kai-shek, urgently needed an air force capable of triumphing in a showdown. In 1936, the year that Chennault's Three Men on a Flying Trapeze stopped performing, the Generalissimo put the air force problem in the hands of his extraordinarily competent, Wellesley-educated wife, who had a knack for enlisting aid for her husband's cause.

The redoubtable Madame Chiang immediately set about revitalizing

the air force from the bottom up. But to carry out her program, she needed a man who could do what previous foreign advisers had failed to do, a man with experience and courage who was a model of rectitude—the opposite of Bert Hall. She was to find that man in Claire Chennault, whose aerobatics had so impressed General Mao Pang-tso.

Chennault was ready for such a challenge. The flying team was no more, and too many power dives had so damaged his eardrums that a flight surgeon had barred him from flying anything faster than a training plane. By the spring of 1937 he was also suffering from exhaustion, chronic bronchitis and low blood pressure. Grounded by the Air Corps, Chennault decided to look for a civilian job. An old friend, a former Air Corps pilot named Roy Holbrook, had already gone to China as an aviation adviser to the government. When Holbrook had come looking for first-class instructors, Chennault had helped his two Trapeze wingmen, William MacDonald and John Williamson, get the jobs; since then, Chennault had heard of China's plight through their letters.

At about that time, Roy Holbrook reached him from China with a proposition so wide-open that Chennault could not refuse. Madame Chiang wanted him to spend three months making a confidential inspection of the Chinese air force. The pay would be $1,000 a month, plus expenses, and he could carry out the mission any way he saw fit. Chennault accepted immediately and was soon on his way by ship to Kobe, Japan, where Bert Hall had been outfoxed four years earlier.

American mercenary Claire Lee Chennault (center) addresses Chinese student pilots at Kunming. The rigorous teaching methods he introduced contrasted sharply with those of the previous instructors, Italians who had let many unqualified cadets graduate just because they came from wealthy families.

MacDonald met him there, carrying papers that identified him rather preposterously as an official of a Chinese acrobatic troupe—a traditional cover for Oriental subterfuge—and the pair had a quick look around two key enemy cities before going on to China.

Early in July, just two months after Chennault's arrival, Japan stepped up its assault on China by launching a full-scale attack on the ancient capital of Peking. Chennault, forced to cut short his inspection tour, immediately volunteered to rally China's air force to the defense. But desperate air attacks on the Japanese invaders met with heartbreaking frustration. Chennault found that his Chinese pilots had the courage to attempt harrowing missions but lacked the training to carry them out competently. The Soviet Union supplied China with planes and pilots that helped to blunt the Japanese assault temporarily, and Madame Chiang suggested that Chennault hire foreign mercenary pilots to fill out the air defense. The crusty Chennault knew his fellow pilots well enough to realize that such an offer from China was likely to attract scoundrels and mere adventurers or misfits, not the disciplined military aviators who could execute the carefully orchestrated attacks he had in mind. But the matter was taken out of his hands in the fall of 1938 when an American businessman, William Pawley, offered to sell two-dozen long-range Vultee V-11 bombers to China. Pilots would be needed to fly them, so Chennault agreed to the mercenaries.

He got exactly what he had expected. With few exceptions, among them the skilled flier George Weigel and the laconic Texan Jim Allison—who was fresh from Spain, where he had flown for the Republicans with Frank Tinker and Whitey Dahl—Chennault found that most of the international pilots who arrived at Hankow to fly the Vultees "subsisted almost entirely on high-octane beverages." But before they could really prove their mettle, or lack of it, their penchant for booze and barroom bragging cost them all their aircraft: Japanese agents in the bars frequented by the so-called International Air Squadron overheard details of an attack planned on Tsinan the following day, and before sunset enemy bombers appeared and blew apart every Vultee.

Despite this apparent failure of Chennault's early-warning network, that system was, so far, his only significant success in China. The Americans called it *Jing Bow*—their version of a Chinese word meaning "to

Burmood, always a ladies' man, shares a relaxed moment with a girl friend, Chinese aviator Lee Ya-ching. The two parted company in 1938 when she left for the United States on a fund-raising tour. Burmood soon found another companion.

Its engine draped by a tarpaulin, Burmood's sleek biplane escapes by boat up the Yangtze River during the bombing of Chungking in 1939.

be alert." Chinese throughout the country began reporting enemy aircraft sightings by radio, telegraph or telephone to a central plotting station, enabling Chennault to put his few aviators into the air.

Much more help was needed if China was to avoid being totally overrun. For a time, the Russians increased their aid to the beleaguered Chinese, but by 1940 the Soviet Union was preoccupied with the war then raging in Europe. France had fallen to the Germans, and England was fighting for its life. Only the United States was in a position to help, but it would be hard to persuade President Franklin D. Roosevelt to provide military aid at a time when America was determined to stay out of foreign wars. In October, the Chiangs dispatched Chennault to the United States to get both planes and pilots.

Chennault was put under the guidance of Madame Chiang's shrewd brother, T. V. Soong, an American-educated financial genius who had raised the funds to support Generalissimo Chiang's rise to power. Soong was based in Washington, where he held the combined offices of Chinese Premier, Foreign Minister and Ambassador to the United States. He thoroughly understood how things worked in Washington and introduced Chennault to Joseph Alsop and Edgar Ansel Mowrer, two journalists with strong sympathies for China and powerful connections in the capital. Together, Alsop and Mowrer began lobbying America's political leadership in favor of Chiang's cause.

Chennault and Soong were aided immeasurably by Soong's friendship with one of President Roosevelt's closest aides, Thomas G. Corcoran, nicknamed Tommy the Cork. When they first met, Corcoran dismissed Chennault as a fanatic, but after listening to him in detail, Corcoran became convinced that he was dealing with "something original," and developed a deep respect for the flier.

President Roosevelt was already predisposed to help China, if a way could be found to do so discreetly and without arousing a political furor. His family had traded with China in the 19th Century, and like many other Americans, Roosevelt had an idealized concept of the huge Asian country. With his approval, Corcoran directed Chennault and Soong to key people in the Administration. But when Soong told Treasury Secretary Henry Morgenthau that China was seeking as many as 500 aircraft, he was informed that asking for 500 planes was like asking for 500 stars; the United States was already fully committed to supplying bombers and fighters to Britain, as well as to its own military services.

Chennault and Soong finally pried loose 100 Curtiss P-40 fighters, known as Warhawks to the United States Army and as Tomahawks to the British. Originally earmarked for shipment to England, the crated planes were diverted to China only after the British were assured that they would receive newer planes in return. To pay for the planes, Soong and some American associates set up China Defense Supplies Incorporated; its general counsel was none other than Tommy Corcoran, whose White House contacts would prove invaluable. To handle other matters, including final assembly and maintenance of the P-40s in Chi-

A ladies' man recruited by charm

When an amiable American mercenary named Cornelius Burmood arrived in China with two Beechcraft D-17R biplanes in 1938, he anticipated nothing more dangerous or time-consuming than a business deal. But Burmood, a man who was highly susceptible to feminine charm, was to meet one of the most famous charmers of the 20th Century—and as a result he would stay and risk his life flying in China's war with Japan.

When the flier reached Chiang Kaishek's headquarters to sell the planes as VIP transports, delivery was taken by Madame Chiang herself, who offered him a job as her personal pilot if he would fly for China. Dazzled, he agreed.

Soon, however, Burmood was assigned to more dangerous missions than simply chauffeuring Madame Chiang. For the next two years he dodged Japanese fighters and flak in one of the speedy D-17Rs as he ferried China's top brass into and out of combat areas. In 1939 he had to sneak his plane out of Chungking by boat while enemy bombers pounded the city. By 1940, he had had enough of China and went home. He flew as a bush pilot and prospected for gold before his colorful career ended in a plane crash in Mexico in 1970.

na, Soong hired William Pawley, who had sold China the Vultees flown by Chennault's misbegotten International Air Squadron. Pawley organized the Central Aircraft Manufacturing Company, CAMCO, with offices in Manhattan and a main assembly plant at Loiwing on China's distant western border with Burma, safely removed from the front lines. CAMCO would also provide cover for hiring pilots to fly the P-40s.

It was not easy to recruit American combat pilots for service in China, and when Chennault asked his old adversary, Hap Arnold—who now headed the Army Air Corps—to help round up volunteers from the armed services, Arnold refused. He could not, he said, deplete his own ranks by encouraging his men to leave for service in China. Admiral John Towers, the chief of Navy aviation, took the same position.

Then the President, alarmed at the prospect of a Japanese victory in China and perhaps also moved by Chennault's favorite poem, A. E. Housman's "Epitaph on an Army of Mercenaries," stepped in and overruled them. To Roosevelt these were clearly the days "when Heaven was falling" and the time was ripe for a mercenary band to defend what God had abandoned and to save "the sum of things for pay." On April 15, 1941, Roosevelt issued an executive order permitting military personnel to resign, sign contracts with CAMCO and go with Chennault to fight Japan for one year, after which they could regain their former positions in the American armed forces.

Recruiters set out at once for Army, Navy and Marine air bases with contracts offering $250 to $750 a month, plus travel allowances, housing and 30 days' paid leave. There was also a private promise from China that the pilots would get a $500 bonus for each enemy plane destroyed. Meanwhile, the State Department, which had only recently sought to prevent Americans from fighting in Spain, began preparing passports for the new American mercenaries—known officially as the American Volunteer Group, or AVG—identifying the pilots as tourists, entertainers, students, salesmen and bankers and, inevitably, missionaries. Missionaries they were not, especially Gregory Boyington.

If there was a black sheep in the fold when the AVG assembled, it was Gregory Boyington. He was to the Flying Tigers what Bert Hall had been to the Lafayette Escadrille and Bert Acosta to the pilots of the International Brigades in Spain—the odd man out, the bent twig among the straight arrows. He was also among Chennault's best pilots, and no man to tangle with in a bar or a dogfight. He was, in short, a combative romantic destined for immortality.

A 28-year-old Marine Corps first lieutenant with six years of flying experience, Boyington was a hot pilot stuck as a flight instructor at Pensacola Naval Air Station. There he chafed at discipline and grudgingly provided Corps headquarters with monthly reports on how he intended to pay off his ex-wife and his creditors. When the AVG recruiter arrived, Boyington realized that opportunity had come at last. Later he wrote: "I didn't tell him that he was hiring an officer who had a fatal gap between his income and accounts payable. Nor did I tell him that I was a whiz at a cocktail party."

Socially, Boyington might have fitted better with Chennault's original International Squadron than with the surprisingly conventional AVG. With some significant exceptions, the other volunteers who assembled in San Francisco to board three Dutch ships for passage to Rangoon during the summer and fall of 1941 were a clean-cut cross-section of American youth. One of them, David Lee "Tex" Hill, was the son of a missionary who had served in the Far East; James H. Howard's father had been a medical missionary there.

Most were promising pilots, but they were sorely lacking in military experience. Among all the AVG recruits, in fact, only Albert J. "Ajax" Baumler had ever actually shot down a plane—five of them in Spain. But Baumler would not arrive in China until nearly a year later, so the AVG embarked on its great adventure with no combat experience whatever. Most of the men were eager to learn, however, and like 25-year-old Eric Shilling or 24-year-old Richard Rossi, they saw the AVG as a chance to break out of the restraints of the peacetime military and gain combat flying experience in an exotic place on the eve of what they thought would be American involvement in the war with Germany. They also believed that the United States would eventually go to war in Asia and saw an assignment to guard the serpentine Burma Road as useful preparation for the coming conflict.

Boyington, somewhat amused to be carrying a passport that described him as a missionary, arrived in San Francisco to join the third contingent. He gave his idealistic companions the once-over and concluded that some of them "were not going for the remuneration alone."

His group reached Rangoon in September 1941, after Boyington and some like-minded comrades had laid waste to bars and nightclubs in Batavia and Singapore along the way. Following a liquid celebration of dry land at Rangoon's Silver Grill, the only nightclub in the rather proper British colonial port, they went north 166 miles by train to the RAF air base at Toungoo, which was on loan to Chennault for training.

Burma was then a key British bastion in Southeast Asia. Even so, England had concentrated most of its Asian strength in Singapore, leaving Burma's air defense to a few men and a small number of American-built Brewster Buffalo fighters. Chennault's irregular AVG recruits would be tolerated at Toungoo until they completed training and headed north to the railhead at Lashio in the Shan Plateau. From there they could fly cover on the Burma Road twisting through the rugged mountains to Kunming, China.

By December, three pilots had been killed in training accidents, and others had left because of the utterly primitive existence at the sweltering teakwood-and-thatch barracks at Toungoo *(pages 104-105)*— once a capital of ancient Burmese kings but now rousing itself out of the stupor of the central foothills only to brush away the clouds of mosquitoes that came with nightfall. Chennault doggedly instructed his men in tactics and put them through their paces in the P-40s, a number of which were damaged or destroyed by fliers unfamiliar with the planes. One waggish pilot had five American flags painted on his aircraft; he had personally crashed five P-40s and thus qualified as a Japanese ace. Even the practiced Boyington, accustomed to three-point landings on carrier decks, nearly wiped out on his first landing because the P-40 was designed to touch down first on its main landing gear. He poured on too much power when he lifted the bouncing plane off for another landing attempt and nearly blew up his engine.

Some of the young American fliers thought that the RAF's Brewster Buffalos were better planes than the P-40s they would be flying and urged Chennault to swap a squadron of P-40s for a squadron of Buffalos. Before he agreed, Chennault decided to see for himself which aircraft was better. He arranged with the RAF command in Rangoon to stage a mock battle between the two planes and chose Eric Shilling—the pilot who had adopted the shark face as the AVG insignia—to fly the P-40. The Buffalo was piloted by an RAF squadron leader who had flown the previous year in the Battle of Britain.

Shilling had been taught to fly by his father, a pilot in the Signal Corps during World War I. He was no slouch at aerobatics, and he quickly bested the Buffalo in three out of three passes in the bowl of sky over Toungoo. Chennault decided to keep his P-40s.

The AVG's pilots, their morale buoyed considerably by Shilling's victory over the Buffalo and by the dashing tiger shark paint jobs on their P-40s, were grouped in three squadrons, the first calling itself the Adam-and-Eves, the second the Panda Bears, the third Hell's Angels. But for all their high spirits, the young fliers were less than prepared when they were shaken out of their sleep before dawn on December 8, 1941—on the Asian side of the international date line—with news of the Japanese attack on United States forces at Pearl Harbor.

Chennault immediately ordered his men into the air, theorizing that if he were a Japanese commander he would follow the assault on Pearl with a lightning strike from Japanese bases in Thailand or Indochina to catch the fledgling Chinese air unit on the ground and destroy it. The AVG almost did the job without enemy help. Roaring down the runway in the dark before their engines were warmed up, some of the first pilots lost power and nosed over, twisting props and tearing off landing gear. In wild confusion the planes aloft were ordered back down and further takeoffs were canceled—Chennault had decided that it would be better to risk losing a few P-40s to Japanese bombs than to lose all of them in the rice paddies and jungle surrounding the field. But the Japanese did not strike, and they never again had such an opportunity.

When daylight came, Chennault sent up a flight of P-40s to maintain a high-altitude watch for enemy planes and told his pilots to get ready to leave for a combat duty station at Kunming, China, about 600 miles northeast. After communicating with the British command and with Chiang Kai-shek, he left the Hell's Angels to backstop the RAF's de-

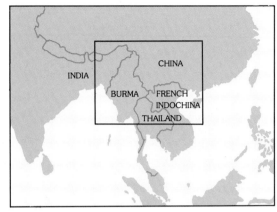

From air bases nestled in the mountains of Burma and southern China, fliers of Claire Chennault's American Volunteer Group sallied forth to intercept Japanese bombers threatening the Burma Road. The area's rugged terrain made navigation difficult and crash landings dangerous.

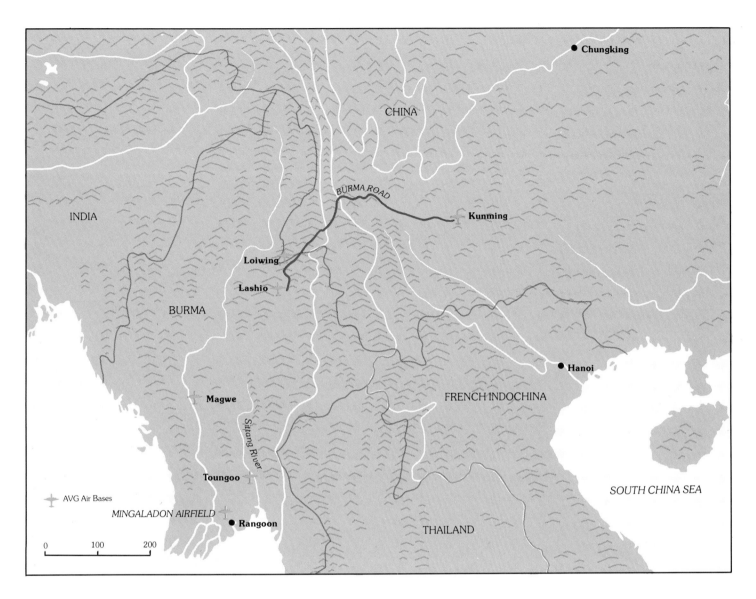

fense of Rangoon and sent his other two squadrons off on their first flight into the foothills of the eastern Himalayas, bound for Kunming. Also staying behind were three pilots—Eric Shilling, Lacey Mangleburg and Kenneth Merritt—who were to follow shortly with three fast-climbing Curtiss CW-21 single-seat fighters that Chennault wanted for high-altitude interception. It would be an eventful flight.

The three pilots took off in their Curtiss CW-21s early in the morning of December 23. But before they even made the some 300 miles to Lashio to refuel for the most mountainous terrain they had to cross, Shilling's engine began to backfire. At Lashio the pilots drained their tanks and filled them with higher-octane fuel. When they were airborne once more over the bleak mountains of China, Shilling's engine started backfiring again. Shilling had flown to Kunming before, but neither of the other pilots had. The crude mimeographed maps they had were marked only in Chinese ideographs and showed little more than the great rivers that cross the high Yunan Plateau. If anything happened to

Shilling's plane, he was not sure the others could find their way.

Somewhere short of Kunming, with no recognizable landmarks in sight, Shilling's CW-21 gave up. He searched frantically for a landing place. There was a tiny patch of wooded, level ground just below a mountain peak. Shilling mushed into the trees at 100 miles an hour, shearing down several of them and losing both wings and tail. Dazed, he stumbled out of the wreckage and ran down the steep mountainside. Coming to a stop, he saw Mangleburg circle overhead and throw down his pistol before flying away. But Shilling could not find the pistol after 30 minutes of searching. Night fell quickly, and he wrapped himself in his parachute inside the twisted cockpit to keep from freezing to death.

In the morning he licked dew from leaves and bits of airplane debris to slake his thirst and then watched nervously while a number of armed Chinese peasants approached. One yelled at him in Chinese, and he answered in English, a language they had never heard. Nor had they ever seen a foreigner of any kind. They decided he must be a Japanese, one of those foreigners who were then attacking their country. They held Shilling prisoner for two days while they made preparations to take him to Kunming. Their hostility diminished only when he dug his wind-up record player out of his personal effects aboard the plane and played the first phonograph records they had ever heard. They insisted on listening to one song over and over again, though they had no idea what it was about. The title, fittingly, was "High on a Windy Hill."

On the third day, Shilling's captors bound his gear and machine-gun ammunition in scraps torn from his parachute and made him get into a sedan chair contrived of two bamboo poles and parachute shroud lines. They carried him down out of the mountain peaks to a village where he found a Chinese radio operator who was part of Chennault's far-flung air-raid warning system. From the radioman, who spoke some English, Shilling learned to his grief that both his comrades had crashed, only 18 minutes' flying time from Kunming. Mangleburg had been killed, but Merritt had survived.

Soon afterward, to prevent a repetition of Shilling's troubles with non-English-speaking Chinese, the AVG developed a back patch with the Nationalist flag and Chinese characters explaining who the pilot was, what he was doing in China and offering a reward for helping him.

When Shilling reached Kunming shortly after Christmas, he found that others of his fellow pilots had already seen action against the Japanese. The city lay among three lakes in a 6,000-foot-high valley. A 7,000-foot runway had been tamped down out of crushed rock by Chinese coolies dragging a 10-ton roller. This was now the AVG's headquarters base for defending China and the Burma Road. Both were in sore need of defenders. Shortly after Pearl Harbor, the Japanese had attacked the Philippines and moved against Singapore. Now they were launching an invasion of lower Burma from neighboring Thailand, moving rapidly toward the key city of Rangoon.

On December 20, 1941, Chennault's *Jing Bow* warning system had

A winged Bengal tiger vaults through a V for Victory on this emblem created for the American Volunteer Group in China by Walt Disney Studios. The Chinese dubbed the AVG pilots Flying Tigers after the first air battle over Kunming in 1941, and the American press soon popularized the name.

received reports of planes approaching from the direction of Hanoi, 300 miles southeast of Kunming. Chennault scrambled his two squadrons, most of the Panda Bears ranging southeast, the Adam-and-Eves and the remaining Panda Bears hanging back as a rear guard and reserve.

The Japanese had been bombing Kunming for a year without resistance, and they expected none now. They were surprised when, 30 miles southeast of the city, they ran into planes painted with wildly grinning sharks' mouths. Using the impressive diving speed of their P-40s, the Americans sliced down on the 10 Mitsubishi Ki-21 twin-engined bombers, machine guns blazing. The reserve squadron came up to join the melee, and soon nine Mitsubishis had been downed, leaving only one to limp home to Hanoi with the AVG's Edward F. Rector in hot pursuit. In his enthusiasm, Rector chased the Japanese bomber till his P-40 ran out of fuel, discovering after he was rescued from his crash landing that his plane had been the only AVG casualty of the battle. It had been a brilliant baptism of fire for the AVG, and the grateful Chinese quickly dubbed the daring Americans *Fei Hou,* or Flying Tigers.

Three days after the Tigers took on the enemy over Kunming, the Battle of Rangoon began with a massive Japanese air assault. The AVG's Hell's Angels squadron, under the command of Arvid Olson,

The voracious visage of an angry shark, with razor-sharp teeth and a baleful eye, lends a menacing air to this Flying Tiger P-40 in Burma. The fliers hoped the emblem would frighten the supposedly superstitious Japanese; actually, it was probably more effective in boosting their own morale.

was scrambled from Mingaladon airfield to confront an armada of Japanese warplanes. Eighteen Nakajima twin-engined medium bombers were in the first wave, followed by 30 more bombers escorted by 20 highly maneuverable Nakajima Ki-27 fighters. Up to meet them went 16 of the AVG's P-40s and 20 RAF Buffalos. A pitched dogfight broke out almost immediately as more than 100 planes dived, turned, climbed and spun through the clear tropical sky above the towering golden spire of the city's Shwe Dagon pagoda.

From the partial shelter of banyan trees, from bungalow porches and rose gardens, and with drinks in their hands from the promenade in front of the Strand Hotel, thousands of spectators watched as the tiny planes laced contrails in a lunatic web overhead. The noise of wide-open throttles in power dives was deafening and it became impossible to tally scores. The Flying Tigers followed Chennault's rules and made their first passes in two-plane teams. Kenneth Jernstedt fatally damaged a bomber with the first burst of his .50-caliber machine guns. A Japanese tail gunner downed Henry Gilbert, the first Tiger to die in combat. Charles Older quickly shot down two bombers, but as one exploded the blast apparently rocked Neil Martin's P-40, sending him down out of control toward the muddy Rangoon River. Two other AVGs, Edmund Overend and Robert Smith, claimed scores, and then two Ki-27s jumped Paul Greene's P-40 and it began breaking up. Greene parachuted out, only to have the two Japanese pilots take turns shooting at

Wearing a cloth back patch with Chinese characters that identify him as an ally, pilot Arvid Olson (right foreground) confers with Chennault at Kunming in 1942. The patch saved more than one downed AVG flier from suspicious peasants, many of whom had never before seen an American.

him as he descended. His parachute was riddled with bullet holes, but Greene managed to land safely.

The Japanese broke off as their fuel dwindled, returning to Bangkok, leaving Rangoon's docks ablaze from bombs dropped by the first wave. Six Japanese bombers and 10 fighters had been destroyed, while the British and the AVG lost only five Brewster Buffalos and four P-40s.

Two days later, on Christmas Day, the Japanese returned. Sixty bombers and 20 fighter escorts came in waves. Squadron leader Olson had been warned by three AVG pilots who were flying a patrol, and this time 12 P-40s were in the air outside the city waiting to pounce on the intruders. Sixteen RAF Buffalos came up to join in. It was Robert "Duke" Hedman's day. The quiet, unassuming South Dakotan teamed up with Charley Older and Thomas Haywood to break up the first bomber flight; they took out one each. Five more bombers went down as the other Tigers engaged the enemy. Then Hedman turned to meet the second wave, scoring on a Ki-27 fighter and two more bombers, then on another fighter. He had chalked up five enemy kills in a single sortie; a mercenary had become the first American ace of the Asian war.

A total of nine out of 30 Nakajima fighters were destroyed that day, and 15 out of 60 bombers—against a loss of nine Buffalos and only two of the Tigers' P-40s. CAMCO's Bill Pawley, watching the battle like thousands of others below, sent the victorious Tigers a feast of ham, chicken, cold beer and Scotch whisky. The celebration was complete

The Burma Road, completed in 1938 by 200,000 laborers using primitive hand tools, winds through the mountains between Burma and Kunming, China. Because the Japanese held Chinese coastal areas, the 681-mile route was virtually China's only surface supply link to the outside world.

Wearing the distinctive shark's-tooth
insignia of the Flying Tigers, this P-40 is
painted with Chinese Nationalist stars
and the 2nd Pursuit Squadron's panda bear
emblem. It was flown by David Lee
"Tex" Hill, who stenciled a Japanese flag on
its side for each of his 12¼ victories.

A venerable adversary

The plane that the Flying Tigers made famous, the Curtiss P-40, was considered obsolete by many military aviation authorities even before it went into production in 1939. Designed to meet specifications originally issued in the mid-1930s, the P-40 was a vestige of an earlier era when low-level dogfights were the norm and pursuit planes spent most of their time patrolling the battlefield rather than attacking high-flying bombers and their fighter escorts. As a result, the first P-40s were poorly armed and could barely fight above 25,000 feet.

The Tigers flew a somewhat later version, an export model designated by the manufacturer as the Hawk 81 A-3, and equivalent to the United States Army's P-40C. The added weight of self-sealing fuel tanks and half a ton of extra armor and guns cut down the aircraft's maneuverability and climb but produced great speed—perhaps 500 miles per hour—in a dive. "Use your speed and diving power to make a pass, shoot and break away," General Claire Lee Chennault told his men. So successful were these tactics that the Tigers shot down 23 Japanese planes for every one of their own lost in air-to-air combat.

Despite their outmoded design, P-40s were produced in great numbers during the early war years while more advanced planes were still coming into production. Nearly 14,000 were eventually manufactured, and they served the air forces of the Soviet Union, Britain, Canada, Australia, New Zealand, Egypt and Turkey as well as China and the United States.

Imitation P-40s, designed to divert attention from the genuine aircraft dispersed around the field, await completion at the Flying Tigers' Kunming base. The bamboo-and-paper decoys were stuffed with rice straw to make them burn more convincingly when struck by enemy tracer bullets.

when both downed AVG pilots returned alive and well: Ed Overend had been rescued by peasants when he crashed into a swamp, and George McMillan found his way home as a passenger in a bullock cart after injuring his ankle in a hard parachute landing.

In Kunming, Chennault decided to rush his Panda Bears south to lend a hand in Rangoon. Greg Boyington remained in Kunming along with the Adam-and-Eve squadron, itching for a fight and getting none; the Japanese had decided after the disastrous rout on December 20 not to try Kunming again right away. But Rangoon was another matter. Japanese ground troops had wiped out retreating British forces at the Sittang River and were now approaching Rangoon, so air attacks continued over the city daily. The Battle of Rangoon would rage for a full 75 days, making extraordinary demands on the small flying force protecting the city and finally giving Boyington what he was waiting for when Chennault moved the Adam-and-Eve squadron down to Rangoon to give the combat-weary Panda Bears a break in Kunming. At 10 a.m. on January 26, the largely unblooded men of Adam-and-Eve scrambled to meet some 50 Ki-27 fighters. But the enemy had now evolved special tactics to deal with the insolent AVG.

The Tigers' advantage had been the P-40's superior diving speed, combined with armor around the cockpit and a self-sealing fuel tank that made it possible for plane and pilot to survive most hits. The diving speed enabled AVG pilots to swoop onto enemy aircraft from above, cut their targets from a formation and overtake in hot pursuit.

At first, the Japanese were rattled by these unorthodox tactics. Despite the greater maneuverability of their fighters, they had been easy victims for the aggressive Tigers. Now that changed. The new Japanese tactics called for pilots to open their formations as the Tigers dived toward them, letting the P-40s pass through without scoring. Then, as the AVG climbed toward the Japanese, the enemy fighter pilots flipped over, executed tight half loops—a maneuver known to pilots as a split-S—and fell on the Americans.

Boyington's flight—which included 43-year-old Louis Hoffman, the AVG's oldest pilot—found itself in that trap as it rose toward the Japanese fighters in a hazy sky. Boyington did not like their predicament one bit, and his apprehensions were fulfilled as he saw the enemy planes slowly split-S and spit smoke and tracers down at him. Hoffman's P-40, Boyington recalled later, "gave all the appearance of a fish writhing in agony out of water." Then it spun out of control into the ground.

Closing in on two enemy planes, Boyington saw one pull straight up and into a loop to come down behind him, guns blazing. Boyington had always been able to outmaneuver other pilots in combat simulations, but this time he found himself in a far tougher situation. He twisted and turned through a violent sequence of evasive aerobatics but was unable to shake his pursuer. Falling back on the P-40's superior diving speed, he broke off contact before he was hit and plunged away.

On his next pass he started 1,000 feet above his quarry. But just as his tracers enveloped the Ki-27, the enemy plane executed a swift turn, and Boyington again found himself the prey rather than the predator.

Once more, he was forced to dive for safety. Returning to Mingaladon after the fight, Boyington taxied up to the flight line. Squadron member Robert Prescott, who had thought that Boyington had been shot down, jumped onto his wing to greet him. Boyington pulled back the canopy and muttered: "We didn't do so hot, did we, podner?"

Henceforth the Tigers would have to fight hard for every victory. And fight they did. They had learned not to try to maneuver with the Japanese, but to spread them out, drawing them away from their comrades, then cutting them down one by one. It was a deadly game that the AVG usually won. In Boyington's second aerial engagement the Tigers knocked down a total of 16 Japanese planes. Boyington himself sent two to the ground in flames, beginning a tally of his own kills that would climb to six that spring. The Tigers flew with an aggressive flair that often seemed to catch the Japanese off guard. The AVG was by nature a spontaneous and unconventional outfit, and its unorthodox flying was a circumstance for which the enemy could not prepare.

The same unorthodoxy on the ground had caused trouble when the volunteers first arrived in Rangoon. The sedate colonial British had been appalled by the boisterous American mercenaries, their drinking parties at the Silver Grill and their habit of strolling about the city in khaki shorts with languid Burmese maidens, sipping bourbon or pulling on warm beers. But after the Battle of Rangoon got under way, local hostility was transformed into grateful tolerance and finally wholehearted enthusiasm for the American roughnecks. In London, British Prime Minister Winston Churchill, praising both the Flying Tigers and the RAF pilots who fought alongside them, stated: "The magnificent victories they have won over the paddy fields of Burma may well prove comparable in character, if not in scale, with those won over the orchards and hop fields of Kent in the Battle of Britain."

But such victories alone were not enough to win the Battle of Rangoon. The AVG mounted a vigorous defense in the air, but Rangoon would be captured by overwhelming Japanese ground forces. In the closing days of February 1942, hordes of troops were at the outskirts of the city, poised for their final assault.

As Rangoon fell, the Flying Tigers pulled out to take up new positions at Magwe, in northern Burma, and in China at Loiwing and Kunming. It would be their duty to blunt Japanese assaults on the Burma Road itself and defend the remaining Chinese stronghold in western China.

It was a spirited, if sometimes impromptu, defense. One night some of the Tigers came up with a brazen plan to strike back at the enemy. Now that the United States had joined in the war against Japan, aircraft from the Army Air Forces—as the old Air Corps was called after March of 1942—began to appear in Asia, and a C-47 transport plane had arrived in Kunming. Its pilot and copilot were down at the Flying Tigers' local watering hole—the bar at the AVG No. 1 hostel. The more everyone drank, the more it seemed that the Japanese in Hanoi deserved to be given some of their own medicine. All that was needed was an aircraft to carry out such a mission. Since some American generals were riding around Asia in bombers rather than in transport planes, what could be more fitting than to turn a transport plane into a bomber? The C-47 in Kunming, for example, would do just fine.

A bargain was sealed and the next night the Air Force and AVG fliers liberated ten 100-pound bombs from the airfield depot and loaded them aboard the C-47. If anyone noticed when the C-47 lumbered down the runway in the wee small hours, no one protested. When the plane reached Hanoi the pilot circled the unsuspecting city and the AVG men dumped the entire load of bombs by hand; then the plane droned back to Kunming. It was said, probably apocryphally, that the Japanese casualties included a general blown out of his bed in a Hanoi hotel.

Such high-spirited horseplay had a military purpose, but the same could not be said for some of Boyington's antics. Not long after the Tigers' withdrawal from Rangoon, Boyington finally ran afoul of Chennault when Generalissimo and Madame Chiang visited the Kunming air base. At a banquet for the AVG, the Chiangs praised the Tigers, who

Pilot Gregory Boyington (far left) looks on as ground crewmen remove a wrecked Japanese plane whose pilot had deliberately dived into an AVG airstrip in Burma in 1942. The enemy flier, Boyington reported, "committed hara-kiri without placing so much as a scratch on the parked aircraft."

remained studiously sober. But as the honored guests were about to board their DC-2 to return to Chungking, the wartime capital, Chennault had his men perform a flyover in Chiang's honor. Seven Tigers—Boyington among them—then roared out of the sky and flew upside down over the parked DC-2, missing it by a matter of feet and sending Chennault, Chiang Kai-shek and his wife diving to the ground, at the cost of considerable face. Boyington later admitted that the pilots might have overdone it a bit. But the episode was only beginning.

Boyington and his comrades flew cover for the DC-2 toward Chungking. Short of the city, the P-40s began to run low on fuel because of head winds, and Boyington decided that it was time to break off and start searching for an auxiliary airfield where they could land. Finally, with their tanks almost dry, they decided to put down in a Chinese

War-weary fliers on a fun-filled junket

When Flying Tiger Robert T. Smith got the news, he made a pithily appropriate entry in his diary: "Hot damn!" He and five other AVG (American Volunteer Group) pilots had been chosen for a trip to Accra, West Africa, to pick up six new P-40s and fly them back to China. It would be a vacation from war and a sightseeing dream for the young American adventurers. "We're all packed and rarin' to go," wrote Smith.

Starting on February 16, 1942, they hitched rides on whatever flights were available. Along the way they bought souvenirs ranging from python skins to ivory carvings and, as Smith carefully noted in his diary, explored the night life in Calcutta, Karachi and Cairo.

At last they reached the United States Ferry Command Station in Accra, where the new planes were waiting, and—all too soon—headed back for China. On the way they saw more nightclubs and American films, and at Cairo Smith rode in a car driven by "a good looking English gal." But desert sandstorms, engine trouble, fatigue and the looming reality of returning to war slowly dimmed their pleasure. On March 22, they arrived in Kunming, China, and two days later one of the AVG's best-liked pilots, Jack Newkirk, was killed in action. "Such news is pretty hard to take," Smith wrote resignedly, "but we're all getting more or less used to it and expect it by now."

Robert Smith (right) and two fellow pilots pose with a tame giraffe in the Sudan.

Sporting the five-pointed star of the Army Air Corps, two Curtiss P-40E fighters drone across the Middle East en route to China. Extra fuel tanks increased the planes' flying time from three hours to four, giving them a range of more than 600 miles.

graveyard, the only flat plot of land they could find. One by one they landed—wheels up because the cemetery was not long enough for conventional landings—and then radioed to inform headquarters what had happened to them. They were told not to bother to come back.

They did anyway, hitching a ride with a Chinese truck driver. Then, in penance, Boyington rounded up some mechanics and went back to the graveyard to recover the planes, four of which were only slightly damaged. After the mechanics repaired the propeller and wings of one P-40, Boyington managed to take it off. He returned for a second plane but then was ordered to abandon his hazardous retrieval mission.

In the spring of 1942, the Tigers grew tired and dispirited. For one thing, the expanding American military presence in China and Burma had not brought the expected flow of fresh supplies and equipment. And the whole nature of the AVG was changing. Indeed, Lieutenant General Joseph W. Stilwell, the senior United States military man in the area, had visited Kunming in early March and Chennault had agreed to eventually integrate his band of volunteers into the Army Air Forces. And as regular air officers arrived to take over operations in China, the original independence of the AVG force was slipping away. The wellspring of wild exuberance that had inspired the Tigers was being stifled.

Boyington was probably the most conspicuous casualty. While he was scrambling one day to meet a Japanese attack at Loiwing, his engine died during takeoff, and when he crash-landed just beyond the airstrip he injured his knees. In the weeks of recovery that followed, his inactivity weighed heavily on him. He did not particularly like China and had no desire to die in combat there. Now he decided that he would move on before the AVG was absorbed by the Army Air Forces. With six enemy kills to his credit, Boyington turned in his resignation and went back to America. There, he rejoined the Marine Corps and later led its so-called Black Sheep Squadron—whose younger pilots nicknamed him Pappy—in the South Pacific. He surprised his critics by winning the Congressional Medal of Honor.

Even among a group of characters as colorful as the Tigers, Boyington was hardly typical. But his departure drew attention to the malaise developing in the AVG. As the intrusion of military regimen became oppressive, the hard-pressed Tigers began to bristle at some of their assignments. First, Generalissimo Chiang required them to fly low-level missions in support of Chinese troops, even though this made their P-40s vulnerable to sudden attack out of the sun by Japanese planes appearing above them. Then, Stilwell ordered them out on equally hazardous low-altitude reconnaissance flights. Chennault, who had been reinstated in the Army Air Forces as a brigadier general though his men still remained civilian mercenaries, was obliged to obey Stilwell's command. Finally, when they were ordered to escort a flight of lumbering, low-flying RAF Blenheim bombers, the Tigers rebelled.

It was not precisely a mutiny, but it was close to one. At Loiwing a petition was circulated among the pilots asking for signatures to support

a mass resignation unless the low-level support missions were canceled. Twenty-eight pilots of 34 signed. One, the lanky Tex Hill, pointedly reminded his comrades that the United States was now at war with Japan, and urged them not to turn their backs on their own nation.

The mutiny fizzled, but it was symptomatic. For a brief but crucial period, the AVG had been the only American combat unit fighting in the Far East, civilian or military, the only one scoring air victories against Japan. The Tigers had been given exceptional freedom and license, but they had paid back that liberty in a most valuable currency—by acts of unusual daring and uncanny skill. Now, overwhelming odds, impossible missions and insufficient equipment, combined with the Air Forces' efforts to suppress their independence, provoked first resentment, then defiance. At last it was announced that on July 4 the entire unit was to cease its civilian role and be incorporated into the Army Air Forces.

For most of the Tigers—many of whom hoped in any case to return to their old berths as Navy or Marine Corps fliers—that was unacceptable. They were not being asked, they were being told—which brought to mind the very red tape, regimentation and formal discipline that they had left behind when they volunteered for the AVG. To them the mixture of total freedom and deadly peril in the AVG was infinitely preferable. And an Army Air Forces general who made the mistake of trying to force them to accept the new status did not help matters.

Brigadier General Clayton Bissell had been one of Chennault's adversaries ever since the early 1930s, when Chennault had tangled with the Air Corps brass over his radical new fighter tactics. Now he was back to plague Chennault again in China. Chiang had expected Chennault to be named chief of American military air operations in China. But it was Bissell whom Washington appointed. While Chennault had been promoted to brigadier general, Bissell outranked him by a critical one day. The Tigers, fiercely loyal to Chennault, resented the appearance of a new commander. When he learned that the Tigers were balking at signing up in the Air Forces, Bissell ordered Chennault to bring the pilots together for a showdown. The Tigers listened to all the arguments, and one by one gave the same answer, "No!"

Bissell responded bluntly: "If you don't sign up, you'll be inducted anyway, as privates if need be!"

After the meeting Chennault—who had remained silent and stony-faced throughout Bissell's presentation—urged the fliers to stick with him. When they continued to protest, he told them: "I know all the troubles we'll have, and more too. But that doesn't count. All that counts is getting the Japanese out of China and winning this war. That's our job, that's our sacred duty."

Chennault saw that it was no use. War-weary, overdue for a break from combat and stubbornly opposed to being ordered around by Bissell, most of them chose to resign; only five stayed on. On July 4, 1942, the American Volunteer Group, probably the finest band of mercenary pilots ever assembled, ceased to exist.

Claire Chennault (left) confers with Generalissimo and Madame Chiang Kai-shek in Kunming in 1942. His relations with Chiang were cordial, but he admitted to being "completely captivated" by Madame Chiang: "She will always be a princess to me," he wrote in his diary.

101

Cutting up during downtime

General Claire Chennault himself admitted that the airfield near Toungoo, Burma, where he trained his Flying Tigers was a "pestilential" hole. "Masses of rotting vegetation filled the air with a sickening smell," he wrote, while "every stinging insect in Burma" infested the barracks. When a scorpion stung pilot Gregory Boyington, it raised a welt on his back "the size of a cantaloupe." And scorpions were not the worst of the thronging pests; deadly cobras occasionally slithered into the barracks.

But even their disheartening living conditions could not dampen the spirits of Chennault's rambunctious mercenary fliers for long. Amusements included softball games, bicycle trips through the jungle to teakwood and rubber plantations, and marathon poker games. Less sedate were pell-mell bicycle races down a steep hill near the airfield. Ten or more pilots would hurl themselves full speed down the rocky, rutted dirt road, risking their necks and wrecking their vehicles to claim a winner-take-all pot to which each contestant had contributed one dollar.

These simple pleasures soon palled, however, and most of the Flying Tigers fled the squalor of Toungoo for Rangoon whenever Chennault gave them a weekend off. There the pilots took over a nightclub called the Silver Grill. After slaking their thirst, they proceeded to outrage the sensibilities of the Burmese and their British colonial rulers by casually ripping the sarongs from passing Burmese women, riding water buffalo down the streets of Rangoon yelling "Yee, ho-oo-oo!" Texas-style, and clumping through Burma's sacred shrine—the Shwe Dagon pagoda, where custom prohibited shoes—in their cowboy boots. Once, when the Silver Grill's proprietor displeased his American customers by trying to close up shop early, they pulled out their side arms and shot down the chandeliers.

Later on, when the Flying Tigers found themselves in Kunming, China, their living conditions were better, but not by much. The 6,000-foot-high city was as cold as the Burmese jungles had been hot, and the food was so bad that virtually all hands had bouts of dysentery or acute diarrhea. In Kunming, the high-spirited aviators managed to while away their off hours taking rickshaw rides, playing with a tame leopard that one of the mechanics had brought from Burma, shooting their pistols at targets on the barracks walls—and, in their nobler moments, trying to help the local Chinese, whose usual poverty was being worsened by war.

On a Sunday outing, pilot Charles Mott poses with an elephant on a Burmese rubber plantation. "I got up and took a ride on him," Mott wrote in his diary, and was "just as happy as any kid." Mott was later shot down and captured but survived the War.

A trio of Flying Tigers loiters on the front porch of the Silver Grill, the drinking spot that came to be the American volunteer aviators' favorite Rangoon gathering place. Rangoon was some 170 miles from their training base in Toungoo.

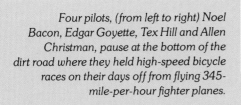

Four pilots, (from left to right) Noel Bacon, Edgar Goyette, Tex Hill and Allen Christman, pause at the bottom of the dirt road where they held high-speed bicycle races on their days off from flying 345-mile-per-hour fighter planes.

Flight leader John Rossi polishes his boots while perched on the hood of a jeep that bears the initials of the American Volunteer Group, the Tigers' official name.

Robert Prescott pours down a brew as fellow pilots William McGarry and John Dean nurse theirs during one of the beer busts that broke the monotony at Toungoo.

Pilots and ground crew share a corned beef lunch under a mango tree at an airstrip near Rangoon between Japanese attacks on the city. The tent served as a ready room.

Mosquito nets hang above the bunks in one of the thatched barracks at Toungoo. The windows lacked glass and screens to keep out insects.

Flight leader Eric Shilling holds a Chinese baby as its mother looks on at the Kunming landing field. Constructed by gangs of Chinese laborers, the field became the key destination for Allied cargo planes flying in supplies over the Himalayas from India.

Three off-duty aviators—(from foreground) James Cross, Eric Shilling and John Farrell—tour the sights of the old city of Kunming by rickshaw in June 1942. Japanese ground forces never reached this remote bastion in China's deep interior.

Three Flying Tigers smoke and snooze inside a shack near the Kunming airstrip that served as a ready room for the pilots on air-raid alert. Japanese bombers attacked Kunming only once while the American Volunteer Group was defending the city.

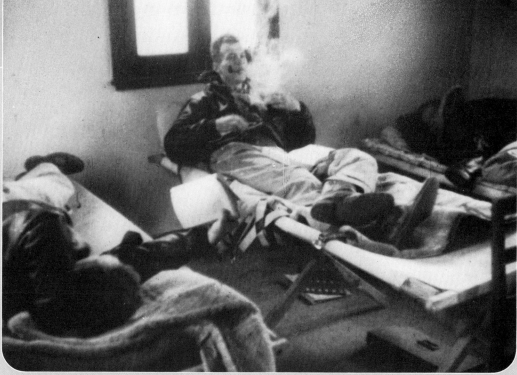

4

An airborne knight-errant

Stockholm shivered beneath an eiderdown of snow in the winter of 1920, and more was falling as the storm piled deep drifts, closed roads and slowed trains across Sweden. Count Eric von Rosen was still determined to find some way home to Rockelstad, his turreted, 17th Century lakeside castle 60 miles south of Stockholm in the province of Sörmland. In such a snowstorm, it would take more than daring to fly. But that was exactly what the count had elected to do. In Stockholm, he had found a brash young German barnstormer, a ruddy Teutonic adventurer who was willing to leave immediately in his ski-equipped monoplane. Since the German had been a flying ace in the recent World War, there was every reason to believe that he could get them to Rockelstad if anyone could.

Count von Rosen, a distinguished explorer and ethnographer, was not a man to be thwarted by a mere snowstorm. In 1911, he had walked the length of Africa from Capetown to Cairo, a journey then referred to with justifiable awe as "the longest walk in the world." Earlier, he had led an expedition to South America and published a book on the Incas that became a basic text throughout Latin America. His was a family of aristocratic adventurers who had come originally from Bohemia, fought in the Crusades and then settled as knights on the wind-swept reaches of Sweden's rocky Baltic coast. One famous ancestor had been a senior officer and personal friend of Sweden's great King Charles XII, another had fought for Greek independence in the 1820s. Other generations had produced leading artists and ballerinas.

With the German pilot hunched over the controls and both men swathed and goggled against the buckshot wind, the plane flew south through the quickly fading winter light beneath a low layer of iron cloud, following the smooth snow of a railway bed through the trackless pine forests of the Swedish countryside. As early winter darkness set in, the stone battlements of Rockelstad came into view and the German banked and landed on the surface of the frozen lake—the skis of the flying machine throwing up rooster tails of snow. Stumbling into the

Enigmatic Count Carl Gustav von Rosen—a Swedish aristocrat who made mercenary history of a sort by flying only on behalf of underdogs—searches the sky from the cockpit of a small plane in 1969. He was driven, explained friends, by his love of danger and "the chance to give help where it is badly needed."

castle to kick off his boots before a crackling fire, the count called for a hot punch of potent akvavit and insisted that his pilot join him for a trencherman's dinner.

While waiting before the fire for the other guests to assemble in the great hall, the German pilot looked up to see a radiantly beautiful young woman descending the staircase. She was Count von Rosen's sister-in-law, Karin von Kantzow. The pilot was so stricken by her beauty that he barely noticed the other members of the family, the count's 11-year-old son among them. In the tradition of the romantic heroes of Germanic legend, the young aviator would in due course carry off the Swedish beauty and one day would name his own castle in Germany after her. He would call it Karinhall. His name was Hermann Wilhelm Göring, and one day he would become Air Marshal of Adolf Hitler's Third Reich.

The young boy that Göring had scarcely noticed that night at Rockelstad was to assume his father's title and become Count Carl Gustav von Rosen. And his fame in aviation would come from a deed so different and startling that it would be unparalleled in the annals of air combat. Unlike Göring—whose path he would cross in war-torn Europe—Carl Gustav von Rosen would turn his back on aristocratic pretensions and become an aerial soldier of fortune, but one of a most rare and altruistic character. He would devote his life to flying for underdogs, plunging into African jungles on perilous rescue missions, hauling precious emergency food relief to remote regions struck by famine. Then, in the nightmarish upheavals of postcolonial Africa, in a murky world of seedy and opportunistic gunrunners and European mercenaries, von Rosen would organize a small strike force of rocket-armed sport planes and almost singlehandedly challenge the powerful jet air force of a warring nation.

Some five years after Hermann Göring's first visit to Rockelstad, the headstrong Carl Gustav von Rosen was expelled from a proper private school, had a fistfight with his father and left home to become an apprentice naval engineer. For a time, he made his way in the world as a motorboat racer; then he turned to flying. By the time he was 23 years old he had been reconciled with his father and had become one of the first five pilots in Sweden to be certified as flying instructors. The young von Rosen began performing aerobatics in a single-engined Heinkel airplane over gaping audiences at the folk parks that are central features of many Swedish cities and towns. His most spectacular stunt was to stage a mock battle with an enemy played by a team of assistants on the ground. He fired harmless rockets from his plane and then was "shot down" by simulated antiaircraft fire: Von Rosen would put the Heinkel into a spin, cut off his engine, glide down as if he were going to crash, then start the engine again and fly off just above the ground—out of sight of the crowd.

While working the folk park circuit one day in 1935, von Rosen

Count von Rosen's Aunt Karin strolls with her adoring husband, future Luftwaffe Field Marshal Hermann Göring. After their marriage the Görings fell out with the von Rosens and never went back to Rockelstad, the Swedish family's stately home, where they had met.

walked past a theater where he saw a poster announcing a lecture about Ethiopia, recently the victim of a brutal Italian invasion. The Ethiopian defenders, armed with little more than spears, were falling back with terrible losses. Curious, von Rosen attended the lecture and was deeply moved. He forthwith gave up stunt flying and volunteered to go to Ethiopia and into the mountains to field hospitals run by the Swedish Red Cross. He was soon maneuvering a tiny Fokker between the mist-shrouded peaks of Ethiopia, landing in clearings roamed by primitive tribesmen, ferrying medicines and doctors. On one such flight, he came within range of Italian antiaircraft fire and was able to escape only by employing his air circus stunt. He cut his engine, pretending to plummet out of control until he was behind a jungle crag, then sped away at treetop level.

After the capital, Addis Ababa, was taken by the invading Italians, von Rosen returned to Sweden to raise money for the Ethiopian resistance movement. Back in Africa, he stopped in Cairo and worked out an arrangement with British intelligence agents, who were doing every-thing within their power to frustrate Italian dictator Benito Mussolini's schemes in eastern Africa; soon von Rosen was flying medicines and supplies from British airstrips in Egypt to Ethiopian guerrillas.

When the Ethiopian cause collapsed, von Rosen withdrew. He had married a Dutch airline stewardess, so for the time being he set-tled in Amsterdam and began working as a pilot for KLM, the Dutch airline. But he had become interested in lost causes. As soon as the Soviet Union invaded Finland in early 1939, von Rosen was off again, this time raising money in Sweden for two fighter planes and an old KLM DC-2 that he converted into a bomber for the Finns. Its payload consisted of two 1,100-pound bombs and four 220-pounders. Addi-tional incendiary bombs and ammunition were stashed in the plane's lavatory, and the bombardier sat in the copilot's seat to use his optic sights. Two machine guns were mounted on top of the fuselage, one aiming forward, the other pointing aft.

Von Rosen piloted the makeshift bomber for Finland throughout the cruel Winter War, probing deep into Russian territory in danger-ously foul weather to bomb the Karelian front and the Murmansk railway. Although the War soon ended with a Russian victory, the valiant Finns preserved the DC-2 in the city of Hämeenlinna as a memento of the struggle.

Returning to Holland, von Rosen passed through Germany on the eve of Hitler's blitzkrieg against the Low Countries. Although von Ro-sen's Aunt Karin had died in 1931, Hermann Göring had remained devoted to his late wife's memory. And in spite of some ill will that existed between Göring and the von Rosen family, the powerful Ger-man Air Marshal was delighted when Karin's young Swedish nephew stopped off in Berlin to visit him. Göring advised strongly against pro-ceeding to Holland just then, but he did not explain why.

Von Rosen declined to change his travel plans. Four days after he arrived in Amsterdam, he awoke to find the sky filled with Göring's Luftwaffe. Dive bombers pounded the city while paratroopers bloomed in the delft blue sky. He raced to Schipol Airport, where a battle was raging, and with the help of a Dutch radio operator managed to get a KLM DC-3 out of a hangar and away from the field. After loading the plane with vital Dutch military and state papers, von Rosen and KLM's chief pilot flew the DC-3 out to England through a hail of German antiaircraft fire as Holland fell. The British authorities were delighted to receive them—until they interviewed von Rosen. Later, he described the exchange:

"You are Dutch?"

"No, I am a Swede."

"When did you come to Holland?"

"Four days ago."

"Where did you come from?"

"Berlin."

"Where did you stay in Berlin?"

"With Göring."

The astonished British arrested him and took him to London, where he was interrogated and roughed up. Luckily, a British official who had known him in Ethiopia got wind of what was befalling him and sorted matters out. Von Rosen soon found his way back to neutral Sweden aboard a Finnish freighter. Immediately upon his arrival, and against everyone's advice, he went back to Germany on his way to occupied Holland in search of his wife. Before he could reach Amsterdam the Gestapo arrested him, but he was able to persuade them to let him make a phone call. He called the Air Marshal.

Göring at first told von Rosen that he could not help him, but then he relented on the condition that the brash young count promise to go immediately to Holland, collect his wife and return to neutral Sweden for the duration of the War. Reluctantly, von Rosen gave his word. Under surveillance by the Gestapo to make certain that he kept it, he traveled to Amsterdam. There his wife insisted that she could not leave her country to go with him. Under the eye of the Gestapo, von Rosen had no option. He returned to his homeland. For the rest of the War, as a pilot for the Swedish national airline, he flew courier service between Stockholm and Berlin. His wife, meanwhile, had joined the Dutch Resistance, but the Gestapo caught up with her, and she was sent to the Dachau concentration camp. Later, she committed suicide.

When peace came at last, von Rosen turned his back on Europe. Ethiopia beckoned, and the green hills of Africa. For 10 years, von Rosen devoted himself to helping Ethiopia build a modern air force, and a grateful Emperor Haile Selassie rewarded him with a coffee plantation in the mountains. By 1956, though, his job with the Ethiopian air force seemed to have been completed, and von Rosen decided that it was time to find a new endeavor, a cause in urgent need of a champion.

Until that cause appeared, he settled for a job as a pilot for Sweden's

Conducting an inspection with Emperor Haile Selassie (left foreground), Count von Rosen (center foreground) tours an airfield in Ethiopia. After helping to establish the Ethiopian air force, the Swedish soldier of fortune became its commander in 1946 and remained in that post for 10 years.

big international charter airline, Transair, flying out of Malmo. His flights were routine. He carried tourists to Mediterranean resorts, or to the Canary Islands off the northwest coast of Africa. On occasion, he flew into Africa to bring back caged wildlife for European zoos. These were innocent flights, marked only by thin white contrails through endless African skies over the terrain where his father had once taken the longest walk in the world. But some of the other contrails in those skies were not so innocent, and when war broke out in the Congo in 1960—and mercenaries and gunrunners began gathering like birds of prey—events began to sweep Count von Rosen inexorably into the centers of conflict.

Howling over the tropical grassland like outraged beasts, multiengined planes swept into Leopoldville, the capital of the Congo, to disgorge thousands of blue-helmeted United Nations troops who had been drawn from a number of member countries. They had come at the request of the government of the newly independent Congo to put down the secession of Katanga, a mineral-rich province in the southeastern part of the country, led by Moise Tshombe. The United Nations

Between 1960 and 1963, Katanga, a rebel province in the southeast corner of the Congo, hired European pilots to help gain its independence. After United Nations peace-keeping troops took Elizabethville and Jadotville, Katanga's makeshift air force dropped bombs on both cities.

forces maintained an uneasy peace for more than a year, but when hostilities flared once more in September of 1961, they were in trouble almost immediately, for they had not provided for their own air protection. The aircraft that had brought them in were transport planes, some of them chartered from the Swedish firm Transair, and once they had landed in Leopoldville, the troops were embarrassingly naked of fighter cover. Tshombe in Katanga was quick to take advantage.

Tshombe hired a force of European ground mercenaries to bolster his gendarmerie in its continuing battle against the United Nations peace-keeping force; to rule the sky over Katanga, he purchased a meager air force consisting of two French-built Fouga Magister jet trainers, 12 American T-6 Texan single-engined prop trainers, some Dornier 28 light prop transports from Germany and some British de Havilland Doves. To fly this collection of aircraft, Tshombe hired a mixed group of foreign pilots, some of them with roots in the British Royal Air Force. Because they met no opposition, the mercenary pilots were able to inflict heavy blows from the outset. One of Tshombe's warplanes attacked a United Nations column near Jadotville and turned it back,

From the cabin of a converted de Havilland Dove passenger plane, a Katangan airman trains his machine gun on enemy foot soldiers below. Polish pilot Jean Zumbach—alias Johnny Brown—flew this plane for the Katangans during their rebellion.

much to the indignation of the Security Council in New York City.

Tshombe assembled his strike force of mercenary pilots and infantry from a half-hidden rats' nest of international intrigue left among the human rubble of World War II. Like each great conflict before, the War had provided a surplus of professional soldiers and vast quantities of weapons. Both men and guns were available for a price, and surplus planes and surplus pilots were for hire cheap.

Katanga's white mercenaries were recruited in London, Marseilles, Brussels, Johannesburg and Salisbury. The principal recruiting office, in Johannesburg, was run by South African Russell Cargill and by Carlos Huyghe, a Belgian pilot who had flown in the RAF. Huyghe was in charge of signing up aviators. Recruits were obtained by word of mouth and by newspaper advertisements that called for "ex-servicemen looking for an interesting and adventurous career." The advertisements quickly attracted attention in the London hangouts of men who had notched their Sten guns on the rebellious Mau-Mau in Kenya, and in the bistros of Marseilles frequented by tough, ultra-right commandos of the French Secret Army Organization that was formed in early 1961 and that had attempted to seize power in Algeria.

Promising recruits were given airline tickets to Elizabethville, the capital of Katanga Province. On arrival they signed contracts for six months at pay of up to $800 a month for ground mercenaries and a generous $1,000 per mission for seasoned combat pilots. The contract included a "danger allowance," an insurance policy, a family allowance, and a paid vacation after one year. Volunteers came from all walks of life, with motives ranging from money and adventure to domestic troubles and a hunger to serve a cause. Among the mercenary officers were also some bent on serving secret political ends, for many regional and global powers—including South Africa, Belgium and France—saw leverage to be gained in the Congo upheaval.

Among the most famous ground mercenaries to emerge were the Frenchmen Roger Trinquier, René Faulques and Robert Denard, all men with exotic combat experience dating back to Indochina and beyond. From England came Richard Browne, John Peters, Alistair Wicks and a Welshman called Taffy Williams. From South Africa came the most famous of all, Colonel Michael "Mad Mike" Hoare, a veteran of World War II commando operations in Burma who had grown restless living in Durban, South Africa. And from among the Belgian settlers in the Congo came Jean "Black Jack" Schramme, intent upon preserving his sprawling plantation.

Compared with these flamboyant foot soldiers, the mercenary pilots remained little known, aloof and secretive—possibly because they flew at times from fields across the borders of neighboring countries and were obliged to hide the exact details of their operations. The shoestring Katangan air force was under the titular leadership of Afrikaaner Jeremiah Puren, who was also one of Tshombe's most active foreign purchasing agents and contact men.

Joseph Delin, 47, also known as José, was the top-ranking flight instructor. A Belgian-born South African with a gray moustache, Delin was a veteran of the South African Air Force. His fellow pilots found Delin remote and solitary—"one of the quietest blokes we have," said one. They never saw him drunk. He lived alone in a cottage next to Katangan air force headquarters in Kolwezi, guarded by Katangan paratroopers, while his wife remained safely in the Transvaal. In the beginning, Delin flew a de Havilland Dove, a twin-engined propeller aircraft with a side door through which soldiers could fire a heavy machine gun and throw out small bombs. But Delin soon proved to be one of the most aggressive fliers in the Congo, and he took command of the one Fouga jet that stayed operational. Delin concentrated on navigating, bombing and strafing, while the two-seater Fouga was flown to its targets by a dashing 28-year-old Belgian lady-killer who was known simply as Magain.

Hottest of the prop pilots was a Hungarian freedom fighter named Sandor Gyurkits. He was called Sputnik because he had fought the Russians in the 1956 Budapest uprising.

Together, this unlikely group helped slow the advance of a 10,000-man United Nations force, with unexpected consequences. World opinion originally favored United Nations intervention, but the stubborn defense of Katanga by the wily Tshombe and his tribal gendarmerie, spearheaded by only about 200 white mercenaries, inspired a backlash. Soon, all over the world there appeared increasing sentiment opposing the world body's intervention in a regional independence movement. When the United Nations force finally bludgeoned its way into Elizabethville, it became the object of growing condemnation. Further embarrassment came when a lone Fouga Magister struck the United Nations troops holding Elizabethville's airport, shot up the headquarters of United Nations representative Conor Cruise O'Brien of Ireland, then sped north to strafe the sprawling United Nations-held air base at Kamina.

To bring an end to the growing conflict, United Nations Secretary-General Dag Hammarskjöld had flown to the Congo to take personal charge, arranging to meet Tshombe in Ndola, Northern Rhodesia, for truce talks. Hammarskjöld was to be flown from Leopoldville to Ndola on a plane chartered from Sweden's Transair; Count Carl Gustav von Rosen, who had arrived on the scene as the line's chief of Congo operations, would ordinarily have been at the controls. But von Rosen was temporarily in Sweden on business. His place in the cockpit of the

At Elizabethville Airport in the Congo, a United Nations soldier inspects a Fouga Magister captured from Katanga President Moise Tshombe's air fleet. These sleek craft were intended, said one of Tshombe's mercenary pilots, "to show we had jets and could control the skies over Katanga."

DC-6B—named *Albertina*—was taken by another Swede, Per Hallonquist. With Dag Hammarskjöld aboard, the *Albertina* took off for Ndola on September 17, 1961. Seven miles short of its destination it crashed under mysterious circumstances, killing everyone aboard. No satisfactory explanation of the crash would ever be found.

Hammarskjöld's death was followed by a cease-fire, but bitter fighting resumed in early December. This time, the United Nations command threw its own air power into play. Six Swedish Saab jet fighters, five Indian Canberra twin-jet bombers and four Ethiopian F-86 Sabrejets had been dispatched to the Congo. Flying out of Luluabourg, they pounced on Katanga's little mercenary air force at Kolwezi and destroyed it on the ground. On December 21, both sides agreed on another cease-fire, and from that moment the war was all but over. Fighting broke out again a year later, but without air superiority, Katanga collapsed. Tshombe went into exile in Madrid in June 1963; not long afterward, the central government in Leopoldville resumed control of the province, with the United Nations forces remaining for another year to keep the peace.

Ironically, when tribesmen known for their fierceness as Simbas—lions—staged a bloody insurrection in the northeastern Congo in mid-1964, Tshombe was summoned to head the same central government in Leopoldville that had called in the now-departed United Nations force to crush him in Katanga. Tshombe's foreign mercenaries had remained remarkably loyal to him and eagerly answered his call to serve again. But once Tshombe had put down the Simbas' rebellion, he was ousted again by the Congolese government, then kidnapped and murdered.

After Tshombe's death, his old mercenaries of ground and air were obliged to seek action elsewhere, in a war outside the Congo. And just up the west coast of Africa in turbulent Nigeria, they got more than they bargained for—a conflict so hopeless and deadly that before it ended even the most hardened ground mercenaries were making excuses to go home. In Nigeria, as a result, most of the prominent mercenary roles were played in the air, by international pilots flying for both sides. Only a handful of ground mercenaries stuck it out to the bitter end, to fight for unlucky Biafra, the lost cause of all African lost causes. Everyone else was much too busy making money gunrunning.

Gunrunning south of the Sahara was big business in the eventful 1960s. In their efforts to influence African affairs, both Communist and Western governments became involved in secret arms deals carried out by private entrepreneurs. The stakes were high and the risks were hair-raising. One shadowy European weapons broker was assassinated by a bomb planted in his car. Another was murdered in a Geneva hotel lobby by a poisoned arrow.

But some pilots were willing to take their chances in order to meet payments on cargo aircraft that they were purchasing. The risks were well worthwhile: For just a few hours in the air with a load of machine guns, a pilot with his own plane could take in about $20,000.

Hank Warton was typical of this daring breed. A six-foot-tall American citizen who listed his residence as Miami, Florida, Henry Arthur Warton was known to his old friends as Heinrich Wartski, a German immigrant born in Grätz—later part of Poland—in 1916. In the 1930s, Warton accompanied his widowed mother to America. Following wartime service in the United States Army, he supported himself as a pastry cook until 1947, when he obtained a commercial pilot's license on the GI Bill. After a series of jobs with East Coast airlines, lugging tourists to Florida, Warton went back to Europe in the mid-1950s. He took what flying jobs he could get, airlifting refugees for an international organization based in Geneva and piloting cargo charters to the Congo for the Swiss air charter firm Balair.

During those turbulent times in the Congo, no one could fail to note the band of international pilots who made their living ferrying secret cargoes into troubled areas for nonexistent firms—front organizations for arms merchants. A pilot could make fat profits hauling such cargoes if he flew his own plane and did not ask too many questions. In the early 1960s, Warton acquired the first of two aging DC-4s on lease-purchase—rental with option to buy.

But the world of gunrunning did not beat a path to Hank Warton's front door; it sneaked in the back way, when he was setting up a cargo line to fly flowers to Düsseldorf and baby chicks from Holland. On a visit to Rotterdam, he met an African poet named Christopher Okigbo, who got Warton interested in the turmoil that was racking newly independent Nigeria.

Within this newborn nation there were three large and antagonistic tribal groups—the Hausa in the north, the animist Yoruba in the west, and the Ibo in the southeast. Under British rule, and for several years after Nigeria's independence was granted in 1960, animosities among these diverse groups had been subdued. But rioting against the seemingly dominant Ibo began in early 1966. Growing desperate, the Ibo plotted to secede from Nigeria and establish a separate nation named Biafra, after the body of water off the coast—the Bight of Biafra. Guns would be needed, and in the summer of 1966, almost one year before they announced their secession, the Biafrans began rounding up weapons. Finding guns turned out to be no problem, but delivery was.

Biafra had vast oil reserves that were currently enriching British companies that maintained close ties with their country's former Nigerian colony. Biafra's independence, and access to its oil supplies, were thus of great interest to Israel and France. Israeli agents steered the Biafrans to Paul Favier, a former senior officer in the French Sûreté Nationale, the national police force, who just happened to have 3,600 submachine guns stored in a warehouse in Holland, and access to all the 9-millimeter ammunition that anyone could desire. The deal was settled by the poet

Okigbo, a dedicated Biafran who had distinguished himself as editor of the West African arts journal *Transition*. He proved to be equally energetic in his work for Biafra. Okigbo was looking for a pilot willing to take considerable risks for money. Hank Warton was his man. He readily agreed to fly Favier's goods to Port Harcourt in southeastern Nigeria, the main port of the future Biafra.

The shipment hit its first snag when the fastidious Dutch government would not grant an arms export license for Nigeria. Favier, the seller, got around that problem by arranging to export the guns to England instead, ostensibly for reconditioning by a company in Birmingham. So, in October of 1966, Hank Warton abandoned his chicks-and-flowers project and flew into Rotterdam's Zestienhoven Airport to pick up his first cargo of weapons. His papers were in order, so Dutch customs officials asked no questions as he loaded the crated submachine guns aboard his plane. The battered old DC-4 took off without further incident, headed ostensibly for Birmingham.

The plane never arrived at its supposed destination. Instead, Warton flew the craft to the Spanish island of Majorca in the Mediterranean. There he refueled and took off for Nigeria by way of stops in Algeria and at Fort Lamy in Chad. Unfortunately for Warton, nobody had bothered to put flying charts of the Fort Lamy area aboard. After going off course and watching his fuel level drop to zero, Warton crash-landed his plane, with its cargo of submachine guns and ammunition, in Cameroon, a good many miles to the east of Nigeria's Iboland. The old DC-4 broke into four pieces, scattering weapons and ammunition across the landscape. Warton and his copilot were arrested by local authorities, who clapped them into jail for several months to await trial for importing weapons illegally. They were convicted and expelled from the country.

Warton's ill-starred flight was only a beginning. When Biafra finally broke with Nigeria in May 1967, both sides turned to secret arms deals with foreign governments. Britain and the Soviet Union supplied Nigeria, while France, South Africa, Rhodesia and Israel supplied Biafra. Portugal, while it sent no weapons, permitted arms shipments to go through its airports at Lisbon, at Bissau in Portuguese Guinea and on the island of São Tomé, some 300 miles off the Nigerian coast. But to move the weapons the adversaries remained largely dependent on private gunrunners. Despite his inauspicious debut in the business, the most prominent figure among the gunrunners remained Hank Warton, because he was in on the ground floor.

Biafran agents based in Lisbon began organizing a massive airlift of arms, employing a fleet of elderly Super Constellations. The first 12 Connies, as well as two DC-6Bs and two DC-4s, were purchased from European airlines. Another 11 old Super Constellations were bought from the Spanish airline, Iberia, and from TAP, the airline of Portugal. Super Constellations were popular gunrunning aircraft because they were outmoded and therefore relatively inexpensive,

Hank Warton (right), whose pilots flew arms and supplies to Biafra during Nigeria's civil war, speaks to ground crewmen at Lisbon in 1968, while a mechanic services his Lockheed Super Constellation. The plane was known as "the Old Gray Ghost" because it lacked identifying markings.

and they were reliable in spite of their age. Moreover, their cargo doors opened inward, making it possible to open the doors in flight to execute an airdrop—an operation that was vital to gunrunning.

One Constellation was acquired by Hank Warton and put into service on the Biafra run—it was only the first of a number of planes that he would buy with his profits from the gunlift. Warton repainted the plane, and a false registration number was stuck on the tail with black tape. Soon to be known as the "Old Gray Ghost," the plane started its new career by hauling 10-ton loads of weapons out of Lisbon.

The Biafra run was from Lisbon direct to southeastern Nigeria, with a refueling stop at Bissau and another at São Tomé. In order to get safely inside Nigerian airspace, gunrunning aircraft had to evade radar-controlled antiaircraft emplacements by "threading a needle" up the Cross River. By flying at night the gunrunners were able to make the trip with little risk of air interception from the Nigerian Air Force, whose Egyptian fighter pilots refused to fly in the dark. After a night flight up the Cross River, the gunrunners would disgorge their cargoes at Biafran jungle landing strips, and the Super Constellations would then fly out of Nigeria and back to São Tomé island.

São Tomé was not the only channel for Biafra-bound goods. Another was Libreville, the capital of the former French colony of Gabon. There were two groups of pilots flying out of Libreville, one English-speaking, one French-speaking. The English speakers lived in the ramshackle Hotel de la Residence, run by a sharp-tongued French brunette whose primary qualification, according to a visiting journalist, was that she could count in English. Enjoying her hospitality were 18 Rhodesian and South African mercenary pilots dressed in proper British colonial fashion in khaki shorts, knee socks and crisp bush jackets. Holding themselves somewhat apart were a handful of British aviators, veterans of the Royal Air Force. The French-speaking air crews lived better at the ultramodern Hotel Gamba, swilling expensive wines and downing fancy meals—but dressing casually in soiled shorts, stained shirts and rubber Japanese flip-flop sandals called *zori*. They were sullen and taciturn with outsiders.

The pilots in Libreville were tight-lipped about their employer and the cargoes they carried, although they were rumored to be flying in weapons provided by the French. Equally closemouthed were the employees of a curious London-based charter operation that frequently competed with Hank Warton's growing enterprise. One official of the London organization was a former owner of the DC-4 that Warton had crashed in the Cameroon. Before Warton purchased the plane, it had once sat for several months at Amsterdam's Schipol Airport while Dutch officials watched with growing amusement as rain washed off one set of colors and identification markings, exposing a set of Canadian markings hidden underneath.

The London concern's vice president for African and Middle Eastern operations was none other than Otto Skorzeny, the former German SS commando leader who was perhaps best known for his daring rescue in 1943 of Italian dictator Benito Mussolini, held captive in a remote mountaintop hotel. Once considered by Allied commanders to be "the most dangerous man in Europe," Skorzeny was headquartered in Madrid and was rumored to be tied to a spider web of international munitions deals, assassinations and neo-Nazi intrigue through a secret organization called *Die Spinne* (the Spider).

Hank Warton and his fellow gunrunners charged $20,000 or more for hauling a planeload of supplies from Lisbon to Biafra. But even for this high price, they could not guarantee delivery. Too many hazards lurked along the way. Once, when Biafra purchased two French-built Fouga Magister jet trainers, the fuselages and wings were sent separately. When the Super Constellation bearing the wings landed to refuel in Bissau, Guinea, it was blown up by saboteurs. The Fougas, left wingless, never flew—for Biafra or for anyone.

Biafra spent enormous sums to support this major arms-supply airlift. It also hired pilots and soldiers—among them the well-known ground mercenary Colonel René Faulques. But Faulques and his fel-

A downed Red Cross transport plane evidences the risks faced by the aviators who flew food and other supplies to starving Biafrans during their war with the Nigerian government. Despite the dangers from Nigerian ground fire and MiGs, relief pilots made more than 5,000 flights from early 1968 until the war ended in January 1970.

lows soon backed out, claiming that Biafra lacked the equipment needed to train and arm its troops. In fact, the mercenaries had been disenchanted by Biafra's prospects almost from the beginning. For, after some impressive initial victories, the Biafrans were being pushed back into an ever-shrinking territory. Traditionally, mercenaries prefer to be on the winning team.

Biafra relied in the end on the German mercenary Rolf Steiner, an expert in adversity. As a boy of 15, he had fought in the Volkstürm home guard during the collapse of Hitler's Germany; in 1954 he was one of the doomed defenders of the French Foreign Legion garrison at Dienbienphu in Vietnam; in 1956 he was with the French forces parachuted into Suez when Britain, France and Israel attempted unsuccessfully to wrest the canal from Egyptian control; in 1961 he was one of the Legionnaires in Algeria who joined the abortive generals' rebellion against French President Charles de Gaulle. In Biafra, Steiner led some 3,000 Biafran soldiers in a valiant but eventually doomed unit, the Fourth Commando Brigade.

The fate of Biafra's air mercenaries was equally hopeless. In the beginning, Biafra obtained through international arms dealers two B-26 bombers, one B-25 bomber, 12 T-6 Texans—armed single-engined prop trainers—and eight Alouette helicopters. Biafran pilots flew the Texans and the helicopters, but to fly one of the B-26s, the rebels hired Johnny "Kamikaze" Brown.

Brown's real name was Jean Zumbach. A Pole, Zumbach was a veteran of the Polish air force's brief stand against the Luftwaffe at the beginning of World War II. After his country's fall he flew in the RAF and was credited with 17 German kills. When the War was over, he adopted the name Johnny Brown and flew for hire in France and North Africa. He was recruited to fly for Tshombe in the Congo War, then moved on to Biafra. Coincidentally, flying Biafra's B-25 was a former Luftwaffe pilot, Friedrich Herz.

Also flying for the Biafran cause were four white mercenaries who came to a bad end during a mysterious impromptu bombing mission. According to one version of the story, the mercenaries decided in the predawn hours of October 7, 1967—after a drinking party that had lasted all night—to end the Biafran War with one quick stroke by bombing the headquarters of the Nigerian high command in the capital city of Lagos. They stocked up with adequate fuel for the aircraft and for themselves as well, and they were even said to have bundled four giggling girl friends into their Fokker F-27 airliner, which had been hijacked earlier from Nigeria; they also put aboard some make-shift bombs—barrels loaded with scrap iron and gunpowder. They then took off for Lagos.

Their plan seems to have been to roll a few barrel bombs out of the open door while banking the Fokker over selected diplomatic establishments on their way to high command headquarters. In any case, they were zooming in over the rooftops of Lagos' most heavily defended diplomatic enclave when antiaircraft guns opened up. The Fokker blew apart in mid-air, killing everyone on board. One of the four mercenaries fell through the roof of the Czechoslovakian Embassy and landed in the Ambassador's sitting room.

With that one unfortunate stroke, Biafra lost some 20 per cent of its mercenary pilots. The remaining aviators, including Brown and Herz, were rendered impotent soon afterward when Nigerian troops overran the key cities of Port Harcourt and Enugu, capturing Brown's B-26 and the B-25 virtually intact.

Now the Nigerians ruled the skies, and they rained cruel punishment on hospitals, schools and crowded open-air markets with equal disregard. The Nigerians were well equipped, with helicopters, two jet Provosts and 20 Dornier 27 trainers easily adapted to military use. Czechoslovakia had supplied two Delfin L-29 armed trainers, and the Soviet Union had provided a number of transport aircraft, MiG 17 fighters and Ilyushin Il-28 twin-jet bombers. One of the Ilyushins was flown by a South African mercenary pilot who was known as Genocide for his practice of calling over his plane's radio: "Hello, hello. This is Genocide calling."

Strafing and bombing attacks by the Air Force of Nigeria were nothing in comparison with the brutality inflicted upon Biafra by Nigerian ground forces. Even a relatively detached Australian aircraft mechanic—one of a number of foreign technicians and mercenary

Von Rosen and his hand-picked crew—most of them veterans of the Congo operation—could not resist the challenge, though they knew they would face being shot at by the Nigerians on the way in and by suspicious Biafrans as they sought to land. But when they began plotting a flight plan, they got little help from São Tomé's blockade-wise pilots, who resented the appearance of upstart competitors who were willing to brave Nigerian defenses for no more than their normal Transair wages. "It was in their commercial interest that we did not fly," von Rosen explained later, "and at least one description of a landing strip was totally false. If we had followed that, we would have ended in catastrophe."

The gunrunners would not give von Rosen the code word needed for landings at night, and the Swedish pilot was in any case unfamiliar with the terrain he would be flying over. So he had to go in broad daylight, making the DC-7 a possible target not only for antiaircraft fire but for Nigerian MiGs as well. Taking off from São Tomé on August 13, 1968, he flew the fully loaded airliner only 30 yards above the ocean, hoping to remain below Nigerian radar and to surprise and pass any Nigerian

When Nigeria's federal forces blockaded secessionist Biafra by land and sea, mercenary pilots braved federal fire along a route that was known as the Biafra run to airlift arms and food from São Tomé to the rebel state. The usual destination of the planes was an airstrip at Uli.

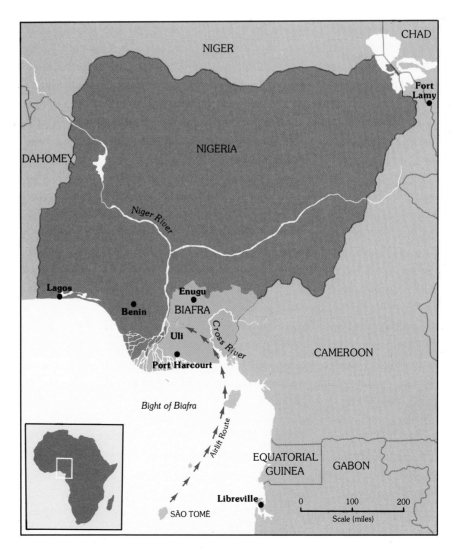

gunboats he encountered. When the plane cleared the low jungled coast and the racing wave tops were replaced by the canopy of rain forest flashing by beneath the wings, the DC-7's crew knew that they had taken the Nigerian defenses off guard and passed cleanly through.

They were almost to their destination, the town of Uli, before they realized it. Von Rosen pulled up sharply when he saw the airstrip, so that the defenders could see that the incoming aircraft was a DC-7 cargo plane, and not a bomber.

"After about three seconds when they didn't shoot," von Rosen said later, "I knew it was all right and we went in to land."

Hardened Biafran soldiers broke into tears when they saw the relief goods aboard the plane. While von Rosen remained at Uli with the supplies, his crew went back to São Tomé for another load, following the course that had brought them safely in. And when they returned to Uli, they knew the landing codes. From then on, they and the other relief pilots could make the transit through the new corridor plotted by von Rosen and land without fear of being shot at by jumpy Biafrans. The gunrunners could not interfere. And the number of relief flights could be dramatically increased.

Von Rosen had broken the Nigerian blockade, but he quickly realized that this was only a temporary solution to Biafra's agony. A fantastic scheme—a plan that went far beyond the transportation of foodstuffs and medical supplies—was beginning to take shape in his mind. It was the fate of the starving Biafran children that clinched it. "I soon realized," the idealistic Swede would later observe, "that every priest, every doctor, every black and white man in Biafra was praying for arms and ammunition before food, because the idea of feeding children only to have them massacred later by cannon fire from Saladin armored cars or MiGs doesn't make sense." His plan, von Rosen explained, "was not to add fuel to the war but to keep the sophisticated war machine that the Nigerians have at their command away from the little children."

Before he took action, however, von Rosen had to be satisfied that there was no other way. He flew first to Ethiopia to discuss Biafra with his old friend, Emperor Haile Selassie. Then he flew to New York in a vain attempt to see United Nations Secretary-General U Thant. While he was gone, the Biafran foodlift shifted into high gear for the first time. By mid-September, some 300 tons of airlifted food and medicines were reaching Biafra each night.

Hank Warton, back at his Lisbon headquarters in the Hotel Tivoli, was meanwhile finding himself very unwanted. Claiming that the Biafrans owed him one million dollars, Warton had halted most of his own flights. Biafran officials countered by complaining that Warton's service had been irregular and unreliable, and they let it be known that they regarded Warton as no better than an enemy agent. There was a bomb scare near Warton's planes at Lisbon's airport, and the Portuguese government discovered that his papers were "not in or-

A Russian-built Ilyushin Il-28 belonging to Nigeria's air force taxies out at Port Harcourt en route to another bombing run.

Hapless Biafrans struggle against a spreading fire following an assault on their village, Aba, by Nigerian bombers.

der." One night in early October he left the Hotel Tivoli and slipped away to Madrid. Those who asked about him were given the impression that he would not be back.

After a whirlwind tour of the world in a fruitless attempt to mobilize humanitarian aid for Biafra on a massive scale, Carl Gustav von Rosen returned to that battered would-be nation just before Christmas of 1968. There he learned that the besieging Nigerians were getting ready to further constrict the flow of weapons to Biafra and destroy the vital airstrip at Uli. If anything was to be done for Biafra, von Rosen decided, he would have to do it himself. And he believed so strongly in Biafra's cause that he would offer his services without pay. He told Biafran officials of a daring plan that was taking shape in his mind and then returned to Sweden to start getting it under way.

In Malmo, where von Rosen maintained an apartment, his son Eric was working at the Malmo Flygindustri, an aircraft-manufacturing concern that was part of the Swedish industrial combine, Saab. The son had once asked his father to teach him how to fly in a small two-seater propeller sport plane produced by the company and designated the MFI-9B. Von Rosen had been impressed by the little plane's hot performance and nimble handling. He had also been impressed by a sketch of the military version, which had been designed as a light attack plane. The unusually strong wing structure enabled the aircraft to carry rocket pods, and the plane could not easily be hit by antiaircraft fire or detected by radar because it could perform so adroitly at low altitudes. It was just what von Rosen needed.

Early in 1969, officials at the Tanzanian Embassy in Stockholm placed an order for five MFI-9Bs for a new flying school in their country. Tanzania was one of a few African states that recognized Biafra, but the significance of this fact seems to have escaped notice in Sweden at the time. An obscure Paris firm—actually a front for the Biafran government—paid $51,600 for the five aircraft. The planes were then flown by Swedish MFI pilots to an airfield outside Paris, where the pilots were surprised to find themselves in a military high-security zone. There, French air force armament experts measured the wings of the little craft for rocket pods, each capable of loading six French 76-millimeter rockets. Then the five planes were dismantled, crated and loaded aboard two Super Constellations. All the Swedes returned home except Per Hazelius, an engineer who was to reassemble the five planes in Tanzania. He boarded one of the Constellations, expecting to disembark in Dar-es-Salaam. But when his plane finally landed, it was on the opposite side of Africa, in Libreville, Gabon. Waiting to greet Hazelius was Count von Rosen.

Two other Swedish pilots and two ground crewmen were with von Rosen. The pilots were Martin Lang, a 31-year-old flying instructor, and Gunnar Haglund, a 27-year-old pilot for a Swedish steel company. The ground technicians were Torsten Nilsson, 58, a retired Swedish air

Relief workers lift a starving Biafran child into a plane for evacuation to nearby Gabon. Nigeria's blockade—finally broken by Count Carl von Rosen—resulted in a Biafran epidemic of kwashiorkor, an often-fatal protein-deficiency disease.

force pilot, and Bengt Weithz, a young engineer familiar with the MFI-9B. Like von Rosen, they acted out of idealism; their pay did not exceed their normal salaries. With them were two Biafrans—pilot Willie Bruce and Augustus Opke, who at only 27 years of age was chief of the Biafran air force.

With everyone pitching in, Per Hazelius soon had the five aircraft out of their crates and assembled. Then the pilots flew the planes into the bush to a secret airfield outside Libreville, where the prefitted rocket pods were mounted on the MFI-9Bs and armed. Von Rosen dubbed the planes Minicoins, a play on words referring both to their low price and to their suitability for mini-counterinsurgency operations. Later, the name was frequently corrupted to Minicon. Per Hazelius was amazed at the transformation of the harmless MFI sport planes into lethal attack aircraft, each bristling with 12 deadly rockets. Then the ground crews painted out the Swedish markings and daubed on camouflage splashes. Von Rosen invited Hazelius to remain with the group, but the engineer chose to return to Sweden.

The first raid on Nigeria was launched at high noon on May 22, 1969.

"We wanted to get them when they were sleepy after their lunch," von Rosen explained. Their target was Port Harcourt, where the Nigerians had a radar base for guiding their fighters. There were also several MiGs and Ilyushin bombers based there.

It was a blistering hot day. Von Rosen wore a yellow baseball cap over his thinning gray hair to ward off the sun. He was 59 years old.

As the squadron of Minicoins approached the coast, one of the pilots sighted some large oil tankers offshore. He became excited at the prospect of sinking them and broke radio silence. Now the Nigerians knew they were coming.

They flew into Port Harcourt low over the trees and spotted a regiment of Nigerian soldiers hastily trying to cover the airport's runway with leaves. All the antiaircraft guns were pointed in the direction of the approaching Minicoins and they started firing as soon as the aircraft came into sight; von Rosen's plane was nearly flipped over by the explosion of a shell from a Swedish Bofors antiaircraft gun. The pilots loosed their first rockets and the Bofors guns were immediately silenced. Then the rockets hit two parked MiGs, and the wings of one of the Russian fighters snapped off and cartwheeled through the air. Next the attackers struck at the Ilyushins, heavily damaging two of them before returning to their secret jungle strip.

The raiders took off again as soon as possible and struck Benin, wiping out the Ilyushin belonging to the notorious pilot nicknamed Genocide, and another Ilyushin, known as "the Intruder," that had harassed the airstrip at Uli.

Three days later they struck Enugu.

"They knew we were coming and had moved every available gun to the airport," von Rosen reported afterward. But the small raiding force evaded the Nigerian ground fire and hit two bombers. "A MiG

Powered by a modest 100-hp engine, Count von Rosen's lightweight Minicoin could reach a top speed of only 145 mph. But an extra fuel tank in place of the passenger seat stretched the range of the plane to approximately 600 miles.

A flea with sharp teeth

Measuring 19 feet from nose to rudder, the flea-sized MFI-9B—the twin-seater sport plane Count Carl Gustav von Rosen used to challenge the Nigerian air force on behalf of Biafra—seemed an odd choice as a weapon of war. In fact, the plane's Swedish maker, Malmo Flygindustri (MFI), had first designed the MFI-9B as a light attack aircraft but the plane had not attracted buyers. By 1964 MFI had all but abandoned the military model and was concentrating instead on producing the unarmed civil version.

Four years later, when Count von Rosen was looking for a low-flying, maneuverable aircraft for Biafra, he remembered the MFI-9B's military prototype. Following his advice, the Biafrans purchased civil MFI-9Bs; then he had the planes armed to resemble their predecessor.

With six rockets under each wing, the craft—which von Rosen called the Minicoin—amply rewarded the Swedish flier's faith. In a series of hedgehopping raids that took the enemy by surprise, his planes rocketed military airfields, inflicting severe damage on the Nigerian air force.

taxied out to take off after us," von Rosen recalled, "but was shot up as he tried to lift off."

Martin Lang had a bad moment when his Minicoin lost altitude and was forced to touch down along the runway before regaining flying speed. But while his plane was on the ground Lang fired rockets into two parked planes, one of them a MiG.

In three sharp, sudden thrusts, von Rosen and his little squadron of heavily armed light planes had created pandemonium in the Nigerian Air Force—and given a badly needed lift to beleaguered Biafra.

World reaction was mixed. Nigeria protested to Stockholm as soon as von Rosen's identity was established. The Swedish government launched an investigation; Malmo Flygindustri expressed surprise; Transair knew only that von Rosen was vacationing. Stories on the daring raids filled newspapers around the world. While von Rosen returned to Sweden to face a government inquiry, his squadron continued its attacks. At home, von Rosen satisfied the Swedish government that he had not been involved in the actual purchase and shipment of the aircraft and had not violated any specific law. Transair agreed to scold him, but only for flying for somebody else while on vacation. According to von Rosen, half the population of Sweden would have volunteered to go to Biafra if asked.

His mission ended, von Rosen settled back in Malmo to resume what he could of his own life. Over the next few months, he was rumored to be back in Biafra, flying on Minicoin raids, like a latter-day knight-errant battling for the downtrodden. In the squalid world of the gunrunners who influenced the outcome of so many events in Africa, he had shown that it was possible to be motivated by instincts other than greed. But he had done all he could for Biafra; in the end he knew it was doomed.

He was right. In response to his first raids, Nigeria had briefly grounded all of its own light aircraft, so ill-trained Nigerian antiaircraft gunners would know that any plane they saw overhead could safely be considered an enemy. "The Nigerians know they are vulnerable," von Rosen gloated, adding that oil company executives were also worried about the safety of their installations in Nigeria. "They know now," he said, "that any day lightning can come from the sky and their whole little world will be ablaze."

But Biafra's makeshift air force was not able to deliver enough lightning to preserve the tiny breakaway nation. While the Minicoins had damaged or destroyed a number of Nigerian combat aircraft, Nigeria still had sufficient planes in its arsenal to maintain almost nightly assaults on key Biafran targets, including the vital airstrip at Uli. Several times after von Rosen's return to Sweden in June, Minicoins flown by Biafran pilots slipped through tightened Nigerian defenses to rocket oil installations, but with little lasting effect. Then the Nigerians replaced their ill-trained and balky MiG 17 pilots with crack East German combat fliers who had no fear of night missions; now neither the night sky nor day-

A Swedish relief agency aircraft drops sacks of corn to starving villagers in Ethiopia in 1974. Flying a Saab-Scania Safari like this one—a close cousin of the Minicoin he had piloted in attacks on Nigerian air bases—Carl von Rosen helped "bomb" Ethiopia with parcels of food.

light was safe. On November 29, patrolling MiGs spotted a pair of Minicoins returning to their jungle base after a raid and swooped down and destroyed them on the ground. Then in January 1970, six months after von Rosen had given Biafra a fresh dose of courage, the Nigerian army crushed the last resistance and the Biafra war was over.

In Sweden, von Rosen kept his thoughts to himself. Gradually, he slipped away from public attention. By 1974 he was again in Ethiopia, his second home, flying food to areas that had been hit by famine. Then in 1977 there was a border war under way with neighboring Somalia, and the Governor of Ethiopia's Harar Province asked to be flown with a relief official to the town of Gode, which was under attack by Somali troops. Von Rosen agreed and made his landing without incident. But that night the Somalis began to bombard the town with artillery fire. Some occupants of the villa where the Governor's party was staying decided to flee; others, including von Rosen and the Governor, stayed behind. Not long afterward, the Somalis stormed the villa. There were bursts of machine-gun fire inside.

Before dawn the Ethiopians retook the villa. Inside they found von Rosen's bullet-riddled body. It was July 13, 1977, and Count Carl Gustav von Rosen was just two years short of the age of 70. ～

Business as usual in someone else's war

Since the end of World War II, mercenary aviators have grown increasingly accustomed to working in the murky labyrinth of international power politics, sometimes flying for employers whose identities and purposes were hidden from the public and fighting enemies whose true masters remained similarly concealed. But rarely has the labyrinth been murkier than in the Congo in 1964.

In that former Belgian colony (now known as Zaire), mercenary pilots fought on the side of the Congolese government against Congolese rebels. But the fliers were Cuban exiles hired by the United States Central Intelligence Agency, flying American-supplied airplanes against an enemy armed by the Soviet Union and the People's Republic of China.

The CIA recruited the Cubans to help the pro-Western regime against an uprising of rebels who were called "Sim-bas"—lions. The insurgents had been menacing enough when armed with spears and other primitive weapons; they became a greater danger when they received modern arms from the Russians and Chinese. "Every Simba in the north seems to have a new gun now," said one mercenary sergeant as the rebellion gained momentum.

The Cubans did the job they were hired to do. Flying T-28 trainers armed with rockets and .50-caliber machine guns, and World War II-vintage Douglas A-26 attack bombers—modernized in the early 1960s and redesignated B-26Ks—they helped keep Simba ground troops at bay with regular strafing raids and attacked enemy supply convoys until the rebellion dissipated in the fall of 1965. The Congo was stabilized, Soviet and Chinese aims were frustrated, and the soldiers of fortune returned to their homes to await the next crisis and the next job.

A B-26K Counter Invader, the mainstay of Cuban mercenaries in the Congo, is readied for takeoff at an airfield in Stanleyville.

Two technicians (far left) arm the rockets of a B-26K for an assault on arms convoys while a pilot and his copilot, atop another B-26K (left), strap on their parachutes. The plane's rockets—and the eight .50-caliber machine guns it carried in its nose—rained destruction on overland shipments and became the scourge of rebel foot soldiers.

Flying a search-and-destroy mission in the Congo, two mercenary pilots scout the countryside for a suspected rebel munitions depot. The Cuban recruits were paid as much as $2,000 per month but sometimes had to endure a grueling schedule of two six- to eight-hour flights each day.

After locating the suspected munitions dump—a group of huts—the fliers level it with a salvo of machine-gun and rocket fire. Similar strikes by mercenaries provided air support for government troops and enabled them to retake areas previously overrun by the rebel forces.

Trapped on an exposed road in a forest near Bukavu, a rebel-bound arms convoy is easily dispatched by aircraft of the government's Cuban-staffed air force.

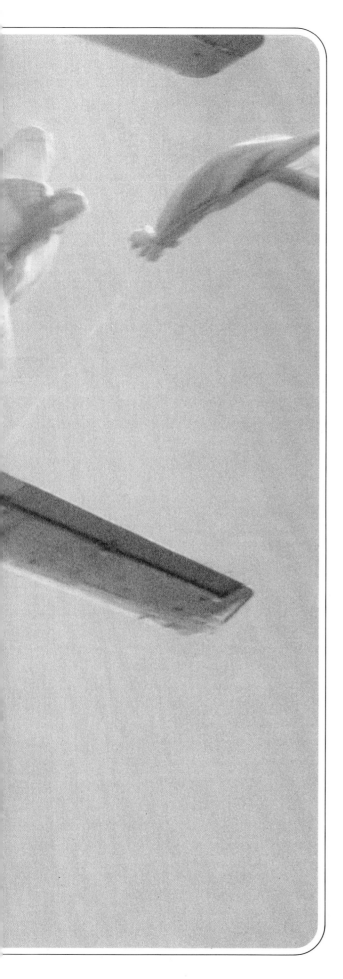

The war that went on and on and on

Against a brilliant blue tropical sea, the coral-fringed islands of Indonesia shimmered like iridescent jewels. The sky was as blue as the ocean, and no horizon was visible. High above the white beaches of Amboina Island, like a distant, aimless bug, a B-26 swooped and lifted and dived again over an airstrip gashed into the jungle, bombing and strafing a row of military buildings and running figures. The nose of the B-26 had been modified to carry eight .50-caliber machine guns, and they were all pouring fire into the Indonesian Army garrison guarding the airstrip against rebel attack.

When the machine guns were empty, the B-26 banked and headed out over the calm sea, bound for a secret rebel base on a distant island, Celebes. Tiny white puffs of antiaircraft fire danced around the plane; its right wing burst into flame, the B-26 faltered, lost altitude, then plunged toward the sea. In the empty sky there was a speck as a man fell, then a white parachute bloomed and former United States Air Force pilot Allen Lawrence Pope drifted slowly down to a coral reef, where he broke his leg on landing and was captured by his enemies.

Three weeks earlier, President Dwight D. Eisenhower had denied charges that the United States was behind the rebel effort to overthrow Indonesia's socialist President Achmed Sukarno. And when word reached Washington of Allen Pope's capture in that spring of 1958, the United States Ambassador to Indonesia was instructed to declare that the pilot was nothing more than "a private American citizen involved as a paid soldier of fortune."

Pope was certainly that. But paid by whom? What made Washington nervous was that Pope—like other pilots flying B-26s in rebel support missions—was under contract to Claire Chennault's Taiwan-based Civil Air Transport, or CAT, a supposedly commercial airline that had grown out of the World War II Flying Tigers. And he was being paid by the United States government's Central Intelligence Agency to carry out air attacks in support of the anti-Sukarno rebellion.

Pope was a typical mercenary aviator and adventurer. He had dropped out of the University of Florida to become a Texas ranch hand,

Flying an unmarked C-123 transport, mercenaries working for a CIA-backed company, Air America, drop ammunition to Laotian troops in 1963. Such drops sustained United States efforts to bolster Indochinese governments against Communist insurgents.

then volunteered for the Korean War, in which he flew 55 night-combat missions. After that conflict ended, he returned to Texas but began to chafe with the routine of marriage and a job as an airline pilot. The marriage ended in divorce, and Pope headed back to Asia to fly for CAT—which had become a reservoir for all the romantic misfits in aviation. Pope flew for CAT to airdrop supplies to the embattled French Foreign Legion at Dienbienphu. When the French surrendered and pulled out of Indochina, Pope and a few of his buddies from CAT went down to Indonesia to serve as temporary combat pilots in the secret CIA operation designed to help overthrow President Sukarno.

After Pope's capture, an Indonesian military tribunal sentenced him to death. The sentence was commuted, and the revolution collapsed, but Pope stewed in prison for four years until American relations with Indonesia improved after the inauguration of President John F. Kennedy in 1961. Set free, Pope left his notoriety behind in Asia and went to work for the CIA in Latin America. But his colleagues, the exotic fly-for-hire, bullet-dodging pilots of Civil Air Transport, stayed on in Asia to continue their fantastic roles in one of the biggest aerial adventures the world had ever seen.

For a total of 30 years, from the Allied victory over Japan in 1945 until the fall of Saigon in 1975, Asia was the place to be for freelance fliers who craved danger and action. Throughout those three decades wars between factions with conflicting political ideologies and between nationalist movements and foreign powers kept the region in almost constant turmoil. Mercenary aviators found work aplenty hauling refugees, medical supplies, millions of tons of rice, countless secret agents, jungle fighters, hill-tribe guerrillas, chickens, pigs and ammunition, for salaries that sometimes reached $40,000 a year.

All but a few of these pilots were civilians—bush pilots and crop dusters and itinerant aviators—who came to fly for the money and learned not to look too closely at whoever handed it over. They saw themselves as hired hands working for "the customer," and it mattered little whether the customer was a refugee doctor, a United States aid official, a family of Montagnards, a guerrilla-warfare expert, a CIA operative or a drug merchant. Painful experience had taught them what it was like to be broke, so they drifted from job to job, flying for Chennault's CAT, or its corporate successor, Air America, flying for charter operations with names like Continental Air Services or Bird Air, which had come into the Indochina war zone in a thrust of free enterprise.

As the military conflict grew more intense, they were joined by a new generation of young pilots flying helicopters. Competitively hostile toward each other, the brash young chopper pilots and the jaundiced old fixed-wing Asia hands together formed the ultimate irregulars, the final expression of Chennault's old International Squadron of 1937. And as the curtain came crashing down on this latest stage of the West's obsession with Asia, as the troops packed up to ship home, these freelance pilots were given the weighty responsibility of evacuating foreigners and refugees from three countries at once as Western-backed governments collapsed in the face of victorious Communist forces. The aviators carried on with the same hair-raising daring they had shown earlier at Dienbienphu, with much the same spirit of adventure that had first taken barnstorming mercenary pilots to Mexico in 1913 to fly for Pancho Villa. But if Chennault had not gone to China in 1937, it all might have happened quite differently.

At the end of World War II, Claire Lee Chennault returned to Louisiana to retire. But the Orient was so much a part of him by then that he soon abandoned all notions of a peaceful old age, cut himself loose from his wife and children, and went back to China. The War had left that vast country in ruins, and Chiang Kai-shek's Nationalist government was now fighting for its life against the Communist armies of Mao Tse-tung. With money from Chinese partners, Chennault formed Civil Air Transport in 1946 and purchased 15 C-46 Curtiss Commandos and four Douglas C-47s for a commercial air-freight operation to move relief supplies to Nationalist-controlled areas.

Chennault launched CAT with only a handful of pilots, including several Americans and former Royal Air Force pilots George Davis and Dave Lampard, who were known to their fellow mercenaries as King George and the Duke of Windsor. Soon CAT's ranks were joined by other old hands. One was Eric Shilling, an original member of the Flying Tigers, who had quit in 1942 and returned to America. He then came back to China to fly for China National Aviation Corporation, but in 1947 he and 12 other former Flying Tigers were let go by that airline. Shilling immediately signed up with his old boss, Chennault. He soon became CAT's chief pilot, and later chief of flight operations, mixing routine responsibilities with occasional feats of derring-do.

As the Nationalists retreated from city to city under Communist military pressure, Shilling flew into Lin-fen while it was under attack to pick up the local CAT operations manager, Jim Stewart. He landed his tiny Stinson L-5 single-engined light plane on a parade ground in the embattled city. Then a Chinese general pleaded with Shilling to take the general's daughter to safety along with Stewart. The pilot agreed, but his plane developed engine trouble on takeoff. Shilling decided to turn back and land again for repairs, but when he circled he found the parade ground crowded with milling Chinese. There was no room to land, so Shilling had to limp away toward friendly territory directly over the Communist trenches at barely 30 feet. Stunned by the sight of an aircraft roaring so low above them, the troops did not fire at the plane, and Shilling and his passengers reached their destination unharmed.

An even more touch-and-go escape involved a total of five CAT pilots in a dizzy game of musical chairs, cheered on by the most colorful of them all, Captain James B. McGovern. Known throughout the Orient as Earthquake McGoon, the bearded McGovern weighed some 300 pounds; in flight, he ate peanuts until his cockpit was deep in shells. He

always landed tail-high—because of his great girth, he could not pull his control stick past his knees.

McGoon had flown CAT pilots Alvin L. Burridge and John R. Plank to Weihsien to salvage company records. Cut off by Communist troops, the two took refuge in a walled schoolyard and notified CAT of their plight. Chennault was out of the country at the time, so rescue operations were directed from an air base at Tsingtao—some 80 miles from Weihsien—by Whiting Willauer, the company's executive vice president. Willauer dispatched Richard B. Kruske to the schoolyard in an L-5 two-seater; Kruske took Burridge aboard but crashed into a wall on takeoff. The next day, Edwin L. Trout flew another L-5 in but broke his prop on landing.

Now four pilots were stranded. McGoon appeared overhead in his C-47 cargo plane and airdropped a new prop. Kruske and Burridge fixed their plane and flew out, leaving two men. Robert Rousselot took an L-5 in, followed by Marshall Staynor in a Piper Cub. Staynor and Trout got out in the Cub and flew to Tsingtao, but Rousselot slammed into a wall in the L-5. Again Staynor took the Cub in but broke his prop on landing. McGoon flew over again and dropped still another prop, along with some empty beer bottles that whistled like bombs as

At Taiyuan, China, workmen put together a Stinson L-5 aircraft for American flier Eric Shilling in 1948. Shilling would soon pilot this plane to Lin-fen to rescue a colleague, Jim Stewart, and a Nationalist Chinese general's daughter from rapidly advancing Communist forces.

Eric Shilling (left) and Jim Stewart arrive back in Taiyuan following Stewart's rescue from Linfen. Both men worked for Claire Chennault's Civil Air Transport, a company—descended from Chennault's World War II Flying Tigers—that flew food and ammunition to Nationalist troops.

they fell and sent enemy troops diving for cover. Plank tried his hand this time and got the Cub out alone, leaving Staynor and Rousselot behind. Then Kruske came back in the Cub and took out Staynor, leaving Rousselot by himself.

Now the Communist troops were tightening the noose on Weihsien, and time was running out. That night Willauer, who was monitoring the action by radio in Tsingtao, ordered several cargo planes to discourage the attackers with small bombs. In the morning, Kruske flew an L-5 in, followed by Staynor in the Cub. Rousselot was considerably larger than the other two men, so Staynor and Kruske climbed into the L-5 and flew out, leaving the heavier Rousselot to lift off alone in the Cub. While all of CAT held its breath, Rousselot lifted safely off at last. Above him in the C-47, McGoon threw a few more empty beer bottles down on the enemy ranks.

By June 1948, when CAT was flying four million ton-miles of supplies a month, Chiang Kai-shek's forces were rapidly losing all of China to the Communists. Chennault airlifted food, weapons and ammunition to besieged Nationalist garrisons, but the Nationalist cause was collapsing around him. And in 1949, when the Nationalists finally were forced to flee the mainland for the island of Taiwan, CAT went with them and entered into a new phase of operations.

Chennault was now determined to do what he could to keep CAT in business and aid the Nationalist cause. He sought financial help from Washington, and it came to him under the table—from the Central Intelligence Agency. As an airline, CAT offered the newly formed CIA an excellent cover for clandestine operations throughout the Far East. So CIA officials, aware that Chennault needed money, used secret funds to purchase an interest in CAT through a Delaware holding company called the Airdale Corporation. In 1950, the CIA bought CAT outright and made it a part of its expanded Asian air operations, now grouped under a holding company known as the Pacific Corporation.

Chennault never let on that CAT was thereafter anything but a private airline hauling freight and passengers around Asia. But the silent partnership was close to his heart. The Communist victory in China had galled him, and he called repeatedly for the organization of a new American Volunteer Group, a new Flying Tigers, to fight the Communists and to spearhead the return of Generalissimo Chiang to the mainland. Chennault lobbied Washington directly and through sympathetic journalists but failed to win Congressional support. He already had a pocket-sized air force, however, albeit one with transport planes rather than fighter aircraft. So he made the best use of it that he could, sending CAT planes and pilots on secret CIA missions deep into Communist territory to support Nationalist sabotage teams and guerrilla units.

Eric Shilling flew many such flights over China, usually taking off from Clark Air Force Base in the Philippines and sometimes penetrating beyond Chengtu, in the central province of Szechwan, before landing at a base in Taiwan. The flights involved air drops to anti-Communist

American pilots working for Civil Air Transport refuel themselves at Tientsin during their 1948 airlift of Nationalist Chinese refugees from Mukden. As the pilots evacuated cities in the path of the Communists, they flew out valuables and precious machinery as well as people.

guerrilla bands and lasted as long as 15 hours inside Chinese airspace.

Once, Shilling flew a DC-4 to Okinawa to pick up a Nationalist Chinese agent who was to be dropped deep in China. On the way to the mainland from Okinawa, he flew at 500 feet over the ocean. When he was about 40 miles from the coast, he dropped down to just 30 feet above the waves, to stay below radar. It was night, but he would stay low until he flew back out at the end of the mission.

On some of Shilling's previous flights, unfriendly reception committees had been waiting for the airdropped agent, and Shilling suspected that there was some sort of leak in Nationalist intelligence. So this time, he told the agent, they would fly right past the designated drop zone, and Shilling would pick an alternative site nearby where nobody could possibly be lying in ambush. Then, after flying on for 100 miles or so, they would come back and the agent would parachute over the alternative zone. The agent agreed.

They crossed the coastline south of Shanghai and continued inland. As they passed the provincial capital of Hankow, they could see the lights of the city go out. Shilling recalled later: "This told us that they knew we were there. I remained calm and unperturbed, partly because this fellow told me that if we had to go down, to stick with him and he would get me out. I believed him."

They flew on to the original drop zone, which was near Chungking—some 900 miles from the east coast of China. Shilling passed it by, as he had said he would, gaining a bit of altitude and then circling back toward the alternative spot that he had chosen on the way in. It looked secure. The agent, standing poised at the opened cargo door, listened for the jump-signal bell. When he heard it, he leaped into the night.

Shilling continued on toward the Nationalist stronghold of Taiwan. If Chinese interceptors were waiting for him, they were eluded, for Shilling skimmed on over the water at 30 feet and made it to Taiwan without incident. The following night he learned how important his secret missions were to the Chinese Nationalist government. He had been invited to dinner with Madame Chiang, who continued to play a key role in her husband's government.

"Congratulations," she said as Shilling entered the presidential palace outside Taipei.

When he had a chance he asked her: "Congratulations for what?"

"Congratulations for a good flight."

"I was not aware that you knew we were making these flights," Shilling said.

"I did not go to bed until I knew that you had landed safely," replied Madame Chiang.

In 1950, United Nations troops were sent to South Korea to halt an invasion by Communist North Korean forces. By 1952, the Korean War was in full swing, CAT had flown more than 15,000 missions

Refugees gather at Mukden's South Field to board a Civil Air Transport evacuation flight. Most of the available space on the plane had been reserved for Nationalist soldiers, so only a few civilians were allowed aboard.

hauling combat cargo, and the line became known as the most shot-at air carrier in the world.

The hectic pace did not stop when the War ended in 1953. Instead, CAT was dispatched immediately to help the French in Indochina. There, after nearly a century of French colonial rule, the Vietnamese liberation forces, the Communist-dominated Vietminh, were engaged in a final showdown with the French Army. In a broad upland valley with a row of steep hills on each side, the French Foreign Legion was making its stand at a fortified base known as Dienbienphu.

The United States was not prepared to support France openly, so CAT was sent in under contract to give covert military assistance by parachuting supplies to the besieged fort. The United States Air Force provided C-119 Flying Boxcars, which were flown by 24 CAT pilots whose habitual uniform was shorts and aloha shirts. It was not voluntary duty: The pilots were told to fly or lose their jobs. They went first to Ashiya, Japan, for ground school and flight training in the C-119s, and then they began flying out of the French air base at Haiphong.

The French air force did not provide low-level fighter escorts, so the

American mercenaries in a Fairchild C-119 drop ammunition to the besieged French at Dienbienphu in March of 1954. "They'd shoot the hell out of you," said a pilot who braved the Communists' fire. "You'd have to make a drop in a certain position and you'd just have to sit there and take it."

CAT pilots were on their own as they approached Dienbienphu. They flew in twice a day, morning and evening. And Vietminh antiaircraft fire was always waiting.

Eric Shilling, protesting that he and his fellow fliers were little more than sitting ducks, suggested making the runs at night, when the gunners could see their targets only in brief flashes. But when the pilots tried it, they were so shaken by the sight of shellbursts and tracers all around them that they refused to fly at night anymore. Ground fire was more accurate in the daylight, but the pilots preferred to take their chances then because the fire was less visible and thus less upsetting.

The airdrops were especially perilous because the Vietminh completely surrounded Dienbienphu, and their guns were positioned on ridges that overlooked the French stronghold from two sides. The C-119s had to make their approach flying down the slot between the ridges, under constant, murderous fire. All the planes took a terrible beating as 37-millimeter shells and .50-caliber slugs tore through their wings and fuselages.

But Earthquake McGoon lost neither his generous streak nor his sense of humor. On his runs, McGoon often made it a point to take beer and cigarettes—bought with his own funds—to drop to the Legionnaires; sometimes he took along unpaid bills to hurl out over the Vietminh positions. He was carrying his usual treats for the French troops when he went into the slot one afternoon in early May, 1954, on an airdrop with five other C-119s. As they flew through a barrage of Vietminh ground fire, crewmen in the other planes heard McGoon's copilot over the radio: "We've got a direct hit. Where the hell are the fighters?"

The first round had blown off the leading edge of McGoon's left wing. A second blast tore a hole in the right tail boom. McGoon, fighting to maintain control of his aircraft, barely cleared the mountaintops as he tried desperately to reach his base at Haiphong. Another pilot asked him if he thought he could make it. Over the radio McGoon's voice came loud and clear: "Piece of cake."

But the plane continued to lose altitude. Eventually it was only inches from the treetops. "Looks like this is it, son," said the voice on the radio.

The left wing dug into a hillside and the Flying Boxcar did a slow cartwheel and exploded, just short of a small landing strip by a river.

Two days later, on May 7, 1954, the French surrendered.

As the French withdrew from Indochina following the collapse of Dienbienphu, the United States became more and more involved in trying to defend the region's existing governments from Communist takeover. American aid missions were established in South Vietnam—which had been separated from Communist North Vietnam under the terms of the 1954 peace agreement—and in neighboring Laos. It was a time of change and turmoil throughout the region. Chennault stayed in the thick of it until 1958, when, ravaged by lung cancer, he went home and died in a New Orleans hospital. A year later, the international operations of CAT were reorganized as Air America, a corporation that remained under the umbrella of the CIA-supported Pacific Corporation.

Not long after Chennault's death, a book was published that fictionally chronicled the changes that were taking place in Southeast Asia. The book became a best-seller, and it would have wide repercussions. Written by William J. Lederer and Eugene Burdick, it was entitled *The Ugly American.*

One of the many real-life inspirations for this novel of incompetence and mismanagement of American aid in a fictional Southeast Asian kingdom was Willis H. Bird. An officer in United States Army intelligence during World War II, Bird had grown close to the Resistance chiefs who became the military and political leaders of Thailand after the War. He had made a lot of money in both Thailand and in neighboring Laos, working as a contractor and stockbroker in the shady world of Oriental payoffs and intrigue. When *The Ugly American* appeared, leading eventually to Congressional investigations of United States aid operations, Bird was one of the prime targets, though he was not a government official but a private contractor. He was alleged to have lavished gifts, including cash, on an American official he dealt with on public-works contracts in Laos. He chose to remain in Thailand rather than return to the United States and face prosecution. American Embassy officials in Vientiane, Laos, would not soon forget Willis Bird.

So it was that the head of the United States aid mission in Vientiane was almost apoplectic one day in 1960 when he learned that someone named Bird wanted to bid on a contract to fly American aid goods in Laos. But the Bird who had come to the American Embassy in Laos was not Willis H. Bird, but William H. Bird, a construction contractor whose company was headquartered in Seattle, Washington.

William Bird had made his start as a rock-quarry owner and contractor on airport runway projects in the Panama Canal Zone during World War II. After the War, he moved his operations to the Philippines, where major rebuilding efforts were under way. In 1959 he moved into the Southeast Asian mainland to begin negotiations on a contract to build an all-weather concrete runway for Wattay Airport near the Laotian capital. While there, he saw that money could be made flying aid goods. William Bird did not care about the striking similarity of names. His only interest was in winning a contract to transport cargoes for the United States aid program. But the embassy official was unmoved. He would do no business, he said, with anyone named Bird.

He had not reckoned on Bill Bird's tenacity. Bird flew to Washington, D.C., where he learned that all aid contracts in Laos were slated for award without competitive bidding to Air America. Scarcely daunted, Bird visited Senator Warren Magnuson of Washington State. As Bird recalled later, Magnuson listened to his constituent's story and then put in a telephone call to an aid official at the State Department. Told that all the flying contracts in Laos were indeed going to Air America, Magnuson pointedly suggested that the contracts be opened to other bidders.

The CIA's soldiers of misfortune

The 1961 Bay of Pigs invasion was perhaps the greatest debacle in the history of mercenary warfare. Branded a "perfect failure" by one critic, it was launched by America's Central Intelligence Agency, which recruited, trained and supplied a force of more than 1,400 Cuban exiles, including some 50 pilots, to overthrow Fidel Castro's regime. Some of the fliers were paid less than $200 a month, plus family allowances. Dedicated opponents of Castro's Communist rule, they fought more from passion than for money.

Two preliminary air raids by the CIA's B-26 bombers—bearing Cuban markings—were to precede an amphibious landing on Cuba's southern coast. Intended to demolish Castro's air defense, these strikes would be blamed on "defectors" from Castro's air force. When the press revealed this ruse after the first air strike, on April 15, the embarrassed United States government abandoned the second. The Cuban air force quickly regrouped and struck the invasion fleet shortly before dawn on April 17, sinking support ships that carried much of the invaders' ammunition and supplies.

Provided with only minimal air support, the army of exiles was chewed up in a counterattack within three days after going ashore.

Cuban Premier Fidel Castro inspects the wreckage of a CIA B-26 bomber forced down at Giron Beach near the Bay of Pigs.

Magnuson was a member of the powerful Senate Appropriations Committee and such suggestions from him were not to be taken lightly. The bidding was opened, and Bill Bird got his first contract.

And so Bird Air was born—a freewheeling international air service of hair-raising flying feats and unbelievable pilots, a bareknuckle operation that hauled cargo, jungle commandos, rice bags and secret agents into and out of the wilds of Laos. It was a fitting name. Only a bird could land on some of the strips that Bird Air pilots used. These runways were cocked at crazy angles on mountainsides, with L-shaped bends in the middle of some, others barely 75 feet long and carved out of opium-poppy fields bursting with red, purple and white blooms. The line began as a shoestring operation, but it would grow big enough to conduct an airlift that rescued hundreds of frantic refugees during the collapse of Saigon in 1975.

In anticipation of winning his contract, Bill Bird had already bought a battered old United States military trainer that had been converted into a transport plane. This twin-engined craft was then parked at Wattay Airport, outside Vientiane, and had been owned by none other than Willis Bird, who had been operating the plane with pilot R. L. "Dutch" Brongersma. Luckily for Bird Air, Brongersma came along with the deal as the new line's chief of operations.

Air America helicopters approach Airstrip Agony, a landing site atop a Laotian mountain near the Plain of Jars. Helicopters and STOL (short takeoff and landing) aircraft were vital to mercenaries flying in Laos, since there were few long runways in the country's mountainous terrain.

At Laos' Lima Site 85, a steeply inclined mountainside airstrip, an Air America Helio Courier taxies toward a downhill takeoff. "You didn't make mistakes," said one pilot, "because if you did you either flew into the side of a mountain or got shot down. People who made mistakes didn't stay very long."

Dutch Brongersma was probably the best freelance pilot in Asia. He had flown for CAT at Dienbienphu, along with Eric Shilling and Earthquake McGoon. A few months later, at the end of 1954, he had taken part in a secret evacuation to remove some of the Nationalist Chinese who had set themselves up as opium dealers in Southeast Asia after the Communists expelled them from their own country. He had also flown mysterious airdrops across northern Burma to Tibet, undercover operations into China and mercy missions to remote hill-tribe villagers who had never seen an aircraft or a white man. Many of the tiny jungle airstrips that Brongersma came to know from Tibet to the South China Sea grew over and vanished without ever being seen by another Westerner. But somehow, as an ex-Marine pilot accustomed to landing on tossing carrier decks, he had developed a second sight for impossible mountain jungle airfields.

Such talents would soon be in great demand. By the early 1960s, the French colonial presence in Laos had long since been succeeded by that of the United States, which was trying desperately to defend the shaky Laotian government from being toppled by the Communist insurgents known as the Pathet Lao. Large infusions of American military aid followed, and there was an urgent need for more and more jungle airstrips, cargo flights, rice drops and weapons shuttles as the guerrilla

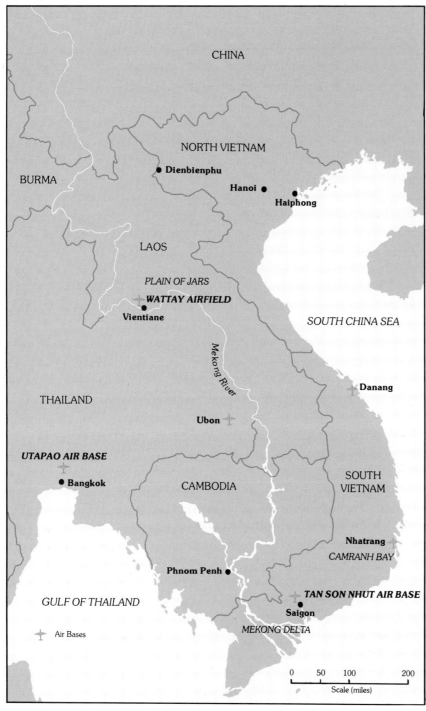

CHINA

NORTH VIETNAM

BURMA

● Dienbienphu

Hanoi ●

Haiphong ●

LAOS

PLAIN OF JARS

✈ *WATTAY AIRFIELD*

● Vientiane

Mekong River

SOUTH CHINA SEA

✈ Danang

THAILAND

Ubon ✈

UTAPAO AIR BASE

✈

● Bangkok

CAMBODIA

SOUTH VIETNAM

Nhatrang ✈

CAMRANH BAY

Phnom Penh ●

GULF OF THAILAND

✈ *TAN SON NHUT AIR BASE*

● Saigon

MEKONG DELTA

✈ Air Bases

0   50   100   200

Scale (miles)

For three decades following World War II, mercenary aviators found abundant if dangerous employment in Southeast Asia as the world's big powers and their client states struggled to control the region. The map at left shows borders and place names as they were in early 1975.

war shifted forward and backward from dry season to monsoon. Bird Air soon grew into a major operation.

The line's planes were specially chosen for the unusual demands of jungle flying. For the white-knuckle landings on tiny strips, Bird bought STOLs—short-takeoff-and-landing aircraft—that could operate from incredibly small airstrips. One of the most popular such planes in the region was the American-built Helio Courier. But for all its advantages—it could fly as fast as 160 miles per hour or as slow as 30 miles per hour—the Helio Courier was tricky to handle. "You had to be with

R. L. "Dutch" Brongersma, a talented mercenary pilot, readies his Bird Air Dornier 28 for takeoff at Vientiane, Laos. Although the transport planes he flew were frequently hit by antiaircraft fire, Brongersma was nonchalant about the dangers of his work.

that thing all of the time, or it would get you," one Air America pilot complained. So Bill Bird bought other STOL planes instead, starting with German-built twin-engined Dornier 28s. Then Dutch Brongersma discovered the Pilatus Porter in Europe. It was a Swiss single-engined aircraft designed for flying in the Swiss Alps. Bird bought two, the first to appear in Indochina, then others equipped with a more powerful French turboprop engine. Eventually, he would buy one every two months, just to keep ahead of the inevitable crack-ups.

In a strong head wind the Porter could land or take off almost vertically, with virtually zero runway. In the Laotian conflict, that was vital; there were no front lines, and enemy guerrillas frequently appeared out of the jungle at the ends of runways and blasted the tiny planes with bursts of automatic rifle fire. Once, a pilot for Air America, trying to rescue what he thought was a group of unarmed hill tribesmen, prepared to touch down on a mountaintop airstrip to take the men aboard—only to see them grab up machine guns and start firing at him point-blank. Miraculously, he managed to veer away without being hit.

Bird was losing a lot of Porters without assistance from enemy fire, and he wanted to find out why. So did the manufacturer, which sent its chief pilot from Switzerland to investigate. By then the footloose Eric Shilling had come to work for Bird Air as chief STOL pilot, and Shilling took the Swiss out in a Porter. During the next seven and a half hours they made 16 short takeoffs and landings at different jungle and hilltop strips. That night the Swiss told Bird: "There is nothing wrong with your planes, your pilots, your techniques or your main-

Amazing mountain bird

The Pilatus Porter—designed and built by a Swiss firm for use in restricted landing areas, such as in the Alps and on glaciers—proved indispensable to American mercenaries flying transport missions for the CIA in the mountainous jungles of Laos. An exemplary STOL (short takeoff and landing) aircraft, the Porter operated easily from abbreviated airstrips perched on steep peaks or cut into forest clearings. A large wing area—310 square feet—and slotted flaps on the wings' trailing edges enabled a pilot to harness the slightest head wind and lift the plane into flight after a takeoff run of some 360 feet. A marvel of aerodynamic efficiency, the Porter could leave the ground at a 40- to 45-degree angle and climb 1,700 feet per minute. And its landings were no less impressive. After descending at some 3,500 feet per minute, the pilot could reverse the propeller just before touchdown, setting up a rearward thrust that stopped the aircraft after a ground roll of approximately 70 feet.

The Porter was also solid and responsive in flight. Concluded one pilot, a veteran of three wars: "I've never flown in an airplane as safe, reliable and predictable."

PC-6 PILATUS PORTER
Powered by its 500-hp turboprop engine, a Pilatus Porter leaps from the ground in its steeply angled takeoff attitude. Sometimes called the Jeep of the Air, the Porter could transport more than a ton of cargo or as many as 10 passengers.

tenance. What's wrong is that out of our 16 landings, only two were on strips that the Pilatus Porter was designed for. The others were so short, so steep, so tricky or so crooked that it is only a matter of time before an accident happens.''

No matter what plane they flew, the pilots faced constant hazards. But they had to fly anyway, sometimes with disastrous results. Jim Campbell, a former China National Airways pilot, and Harry Reno, who had flown for the Korean national airline, flew into a cloud after a rice drop in a Bird C-46. There was a mountain inside.

Jim Fore had the most spectacular crash. He was in a surplus Navy PV-2 bomber that had been converted to a transport plane, and he neglected to make sure that the right smoke signals and code number markers had been placed on a remote strip before he went in. The enemy had taken the field and was waiting to greet him with a barrage of antiaircraft fire. The PV-2 burst into flame, and everyone on board parachuted but Jim Fore. He could not get out of the cockpit because the passage was blazing. As Fore struggled up through the narrow overhead hatch his chute caught; then he saw that the plane was approaching a hill at terrific speed. Frantic, he yanked his rip cord, and the opening chute jerked him out of the hatch. The plane hit and exploded as Fore swung to the right on his chute. On his second swing, back to the

Smoke pours from the wreckage of a Pilatus Porter that crashed just seconds after takeoff from Vientiane, Laos, in 1963. The pilot—who had been undergoing a flight test in the hope of securing a job with Bird Air—suffered severe burns but miraculously survived the crash.

left, his feet touched solid ground. He had landed only 100 yards from the flaming wreckage of his plane.

Fore's plane was one of only two aircraft that Bird Air would lose to enemy fire during 15 years in Laos. The other was a Camair whose pilot got lost and was shot down over enemy territory. What happened to the pilot was never known, but his wing tanks were displayed as trophies in the Communist North Vietnamese capital of Hanoi.

The 22 other Bird aircraft lost in Laos went down because of pilot error—usually a misjudgment of impossible airstrips and worse weather over awful terrain. But to the pilots, the risks were worth the money—some made as much as $50,000 per year—and the thrills.

By 1965, however, Bird Air had taken such heavy losses in aircraft that it lost its insurance coverage. The built-in hazards of flying in Laos were not the only reasons. The caliber of pilots had also changed, and the new pilots coming to fly freelance were not working out. At first they seemed to be hot pilots—a number of them were former crop dusters. But many turned out to lack the fundamentals of airmanship needed for survival in Laos. Here there were no navigational aids: Pilots had to learn the terrain and unusual weather quickly, to watch the signals closely, to be on the alert for the enemy. It was seat-of-the-pants flying at its most demanding. Even for old hands, like Shilling and Brongersma, it was difficult; for many of the new men, it was impossible.

Bill Bird knew his operation could not profitably continue for long without insurance. Luckily, he was soon presented with a graceful—and profitable—alternative. By the terms of an agreement between the United States and the Soviet Union, the United States Air Force had no bases in Laos. Air Force fighter-bombers and helicopters operating from across the Mekong River in Thailand or from Vietnam hit targets inside Laos. But "normal" air operations in that war-torn country—if anything in Laos was normal—were restricted to civilian charter airlines.

Bird Air and the CIA-controlled Air America were splitting the American government contracts between them, but Robert F. Six, the energetic president of Los Angeles-based Continental Airlines, had taken an interest in the Laotian operations. Air America's CIA connection was an open secret in the airline business, and Bob Six believed that since the line was really owned by a federal agency, it was competing unfairly for government contracts. Continental already had Military Air Transport System contracts to fly troops to Vietnam, and Six wanted to expand in Asia and win a transpacific commercial airline route. He hired Pierre Salinger, who had been President John F. Kennedy's press secretary, to lobby on Continental's behalf. In 1965 the CIA permitted Six to start Continental Air Services as a private contractor in Laos. Six then offered Bird $4.2 million for Bird Air. Bird accepted, and the shoestring jungle cargo operation became part of the corporate big time.

Bird's pilots, including Dutch Brongersma, stayed on with Continental Air Services. The newly expanded operation was run by Brongersma and Bob Rousselot, the CAT pilot who had been the last one out in the musical-chairs escape at Weihsien in 1948. Bill Bird continued building airfields, but he stayed away from fixed-wing flying. Three years later he started a new Bird Air, but this time it was a helicopter operation only. It was a lot simpler going into a remote jungle airstrip in a chopper.

Whether they flew helicopters or airplanes, most of the civilian pilots working in Indochina had little real interest in the cloak-and-dagger aspect of some of their operations. To them, covert CIA agents were just customers, of little interest except when they had to be flown some-where. But while the flying job itself was usually straightforward, the CIA involvement often complicated matters. Sometimes, even the hiring process became bizarre.

Neil Hansen had been a bush pilot in Canada and was flying an executive aircraft for Teamsters Union President James R. Hoffa when he decided in the mid-1960s to get a job overseas with Air America. He received no reply to his letter of application, so he telephoned the airline's front office in Washington and was told that Air America was not hiring. The next day, however, Hansen received a call from the airline's personnel manager.

"When can you leave?" he asked.

"I have to give two weeks' notice," Hansen replied.

"Good. I have a couple of questions," the personnel man said. "Can you fly good?"

"I was in Washington yesterday and I'm in Chicago today, and I flew all the way," Hansen answered, wondering if it was all a joke.

"Do you drink a lot?"

"I'm sober now and I have to fly back."

"Okay, we'll send you the tickets and some money," said the man from Air America.

Hansen asked if they wanted to interview him in Washington. He was told that would be unnecessary.

Hansen was something of an eccentric, and when he reached Laos he fitted right in—for a brief time, in fact, he became a Buddhist monk. The pilots found the War confusing and their own living conditions almost equally so. Vientiane was like a Wild West frontier town. The pilots liked the Laotians, regarding them affectionately or irreverently, as if they were Lilliputians. Whiskey and gin were less than two dollars a bottle at the American military bases in Indochina that the pilots visited, and off-duty aviators careered around Vientiane with armloads of pliant Laotian women from the White Rose or Madame Lulu's. There was a 12-hour "bottle-to-throttle" rule for pilots, but it was at times ignored, along with a regulation that forbade carrying firearms aloft; some of the fliers tucked Israeli Uzi submachine guns in their cockpits.

Flying in Laos was a chance to recapture the free-form flying of the Red Baron's day. In the age of lumbering jets and complex electronic aids, piloting a Pilatus Porter was as close as a man could get to flying a Fokker Dr.I or a Sopwith Camel. Hansen took to his new job so quick-ly and easily, and was so idiosyncratic and flamboyant, that he was appreciatively named Weird by his comrades; eventually, he served as a model for a character of the same nickname in John Clark Pratt's thinly disguised novel of the Laotian War, *The Laotian Fragments.* Hansen was seldom without a pair of dark glasses, wore his hair long and sported a gold bracelet as well as the gold Rolex watch that seemed to be worn by all Air America pilots in Laos—presumably for trade if they were captured.

Older hands than Weird Hansen were just as colorful. Among the former Flying Tigers from World War II days was Art Wilson, who had flown cargo on the treacherous Hump route over the Himalayas between China and India. He was known as Shower Shoes for his habit of wearing rubber-thonged sandals while in the air. Wilson had been born in China, had grown up there and had remained in Asia, first with CAT, then with Air America, to accumulate 15,000 hours in C-46s. He also had an Oriental passion for *baluts,* the unhatched baby ducks, steamed in the shell and eaten whole, that are considered a delicacy in the Philippines.

Wilson and other old hands, like Eric Shilling and Dutch Brongersma, were regarded as dinosaurs from a bygone age by the hotshot young helicopter pilots who came to fly freelance for Air America and Bird Air after serving with the Marines in Vietnam. The chopper pilots stuck together, preferring Vientiane's Apollo Hotel, which boasted one of the only two elevators in all of Laos, to the quiet homes and apartments where most of the older pilots stayed. If the old hands were characteristically reserved and went about their drinking with quiet concentration, the chopper pilots were as raucous as a tree full of chattering monkeys. They resented the tired, knowing air of the oldtimers and considered them out of touch with modern combat. They felt that they themselves were on the leading edge of technology, and while they cheerfully admitted to being mercenaries, they thought themselves a cut above other soldiers of fortune, because they would not fly only for money or for just any cause. They would have found it hard to do what they were doing if they were being paid by a country other than their own.

Even so, they knew the value of a dollar. "Most guys believed that they were saving the world," remarked one of the chopper pilots, "but they wouldn't have done it for only a thousand a month. It's a lot easier to save the world for four."

In spite of this generation gap, it was understood that when a flier went down—fixed-wing or rotor—his fellow pilots would risk everything to save him. The risk, and the bullet holes, were always there.

"You never knew how you got them, where you got them, when or anything else," marveled combat-seasoned Bob Dawson. "There were times in World War II when you went to dive-bomb a city and there was great danger from antiaircraft fire for a few minutes, but the hour and a half you spent getting there and the hour and a half you spent getting back involved relatively little risk. Air America was a sustained, day-in and day-out operation that went on year after year. In Laos, for six, eight, or ten hours a day for maybe eight years, every landing, every takeoff, every departure and every letdown and every flight was a risk."

The risks multiplied even further after American and South Vietnamese troops invaded Cambodia in 1970. Up to that point the United States had been fighting an open war in Vietnam and a secret war in neighboring Laos. Now the War was expanded to include Cambodia. But instead of marking an improvement in American fortunes, Cambodia was the beginning of the end. The whole tide of the war in Indochina began to shift against the United States and against the governments that it supported in Vientiane, Saigon and, now, in Phnom Penh. In Laos the Communists began a drive that resisted every American effort to turn it back. The North Vietnamese and Viet Cong relentlessly expanded their control in South Vietnam. In Cambodia, counterattacking Communist forces gradually spread across the countryside and ringed Phnom Penh, bottling up the government forces and the small contingent of American diplomats and military advisers there.

The only way to send military equipment and food supplies to the besieged city was by ship and barge convoy up the Mekong River from the still-secure Saigon area. And that route came under devastating Communist rocket and artillery fire from both riverbanks. When the iron ring around Phnom Penh began to tighten, the city turned desperately to the air, and to a chicken coop of bedraggled air charter outfits.

Even Weird Hansen acknowledged that the Cambodian operation was "a real weird setup." In the late 1960s, Hansen had taken his earnings from Laos and gone off to start a ranch in New Zealand, but the project had gone awry—as happens often when mercenary pilots try to settle down on the ground. Broke again, he had come back to Indochina and ended up flying a C-46 in Cambodia for an operation that bore the curious name of Work Together Airline.

"Anybody who wanted to apply for an airline certificate could get one from the government," Hansen commented later. "The military needed airlifts. Chinese shippers controlled the produce market, and they could not use the roads for their trucks anymore, so they needed airlines, too. The only thing was, they didn't know one end of an airplane from the other." Airline operators bought junk aircraft and for lack of proper materials patched them with flattened aluminum beer cans. Hansen's C-46 had magnetos worn so thin that when on the ground he could get up to only 80 miles per hour in an aircraft with a minimum safe takeoff speed of 106 miles per hour. Once he was aloft, his flying speed and altitude remained low, which made him grateful that so many Communist insurgents were bad shots.

By the fall of 1974, Communist gunners had improved their aim and were becoming so effective along both banks of the Mekong that it was clearly only a matter of time before the life line of river shipping from Saigon would be cut for good. Then all efforts to sustain the Phnom Penh regime would be futile—unless a massive airlift could be started immediately. In Bangkok, United States military commanders held a

Air America pilots unload wounded soldiers of the CIA-backed Laotian army at a field hospital in 1972. The airline acknowledged its humanitarian deeds in Laos—drops of rice, blankets and medicine—but never mentioned its "hard rice" drops of bombs, guns, grenades and other weapons.

William H. Bird (left), founder of Bird Air, confers with an Air Force officer in Thailand in March of 1975. After discontented mercenaries exposed the involvement of Air America in the Southeast Asian fighting, the United States engaged Bird's firm to fly supplies to anti-Communist forces.

series of emergency meetings. Then they sent a car across town to pick up Bill Bird at the offices of his construction and helicopter companies.

The Pentagon was in a dilemma. The generals did not want to let Phnom Penh collapse, but they had few options. The United States Congress, angry over the conduct of the War, had barred the Pentagon from introducing American forces into Cambodia. The Air Force could not mount a Berlin-type airlift. The repercussions in Washington would have been deafening. Air America was out. By then it was clearly identified with the CIA and was widely known to be government-owned. Also out was Continental Air Services, which, because it was flying countless government contracts in Laos and Vietnam, had also come to be closely identified with the CIA. But Bill Bird was a private construction contractor who had been out of fixed-wing air operations for nearly 10 years.

The generals put it to him simply: If the Pentagon provided giant C-130 cargo aircraft on loan, with all military markings removed, could Bill Bird organize civilian pilots to fly them and immediately start a massive civilian airlift to Phnom Penh? The huge United States Air Force base at Utapao, Thailand, would be placed at his disposal. Loading and unloading would be handled by specially trained ground crews.

Bird agreed to give it a try, and he began hiring immediately. Most of the pilots were ex-Air Force officers. "It wasn't easy to find anyone else who could fly C-130s," Bird told curious reporters later. Some, like Chris Rice, had flown for commercial airlines in the meantime and then joined the new Bird Air for the high pay—up to $4,500 a month.

Three times a day, Rice and nine other pilots took off from Utapao in their unarmed C-130s, each hauling 25 tons of ammunition, fuel and food to the stricken Cambodian capital and other government outposts. By January of 1975 the Mekong River supply route had been cut, the convoys of barges had ceased and the Phnom Penh airport was under continual fire as the Communists closed in.

To avoid being shot down, Rice and the others followed a desperate flight pattern. They stayed at high altitude, out of range, until they were directly over the airfield. Then they spiraled down, watching warily for other aircraft. A crew member holding a flare pistol was constantly on alert for enemy SA-7 heat-seeking missiles, which were clearly visible when they streaked up in a corkscrew flight path. When a missile was fired, the crewman would discharge a flare; as it fell slowly downward, it drew the missile away from the aircraft. Because of enemy rockets, being on the ground was as dangerous as being in the air over the field. When the pilot dropped the craft onto the landing strip, he taxied quickly to the terminal area, where a fleet of forklift trucks waited to remove his cargo, which had been loaded on pallets. The engines were kept running; it took as little as four minutes to empty all 25 tons. Then the C-130 would roar back to Thailand.

Each day, 10 C-130s flew three shifts—making 30 flights a day to carry in a total of 750 tons of precious supplies. But it was not enough. Phnom Penh was doomed—and so were Saigon and Vien-

tiane. While the Phnom Penh airlift struggled on, Bill Bird was called in again. This time he was told that he had earned himself an even bigger job: He was to help evacuate three countries. In Saigon Bird Air would join Air America, Continental and half a dozen other American charter airlines to lift out refugees fleeing the advancing North Vietnamese. In Laos, Bird Air would be left with the job of bringing out the last loads of American diplomats and the last of the Meo guerrilla forces from the Plain of Jars. In Cambodia, Bird Air would leave behind only those embassy staff members who could be evacuated at the last minute by helicopter.

Panic stampeded the refugees at the mid-coastal South Vietnamese city of Nhatrang, and they swarmed over the rescue aircraft, fighting to get aboard. Some milled into whirling propellers. At Danang, farther to the north, the scene was much worse. Once, desperate refugees clung to the landing gear even as a plane took off, only to be crushed in the wheel bays or frozen to death when the aircraft reached high altitude.

Bill Bird masterminded his far-flung operations from Saigon's Tan Son Nhut airfield. His greatest fear was that his planes might be commandeered by South Vietnamese troops desperate to escape. So each night, after hauling thousands of refugees southward, his aircraft headed off for Hong Kong, Bangkok or Singapore. They came back every morning, loaded with rice that they took to an offshore island for refu-

As their city falls to the Communists in April 1975, Saigon residents clamber to the roof of a downtown building where an Air America helicopter awaits them. In the final days of the War, Air America and Bird Air (opposite) evacuated thousands of Americans and South Vietnamese.

Determined to lighten his plane for takeoff, an American copilot strikes a Vietnamese refugee who is clinging to a Bird Air DC-6. "We would close the doors," a rescue pilot recalled, "and people would hoist one another up onto the wings and beat on the windows trying to get in."

gees already streaming down the coast in open boats. After depositing their rice cargoes, the planes shuttled refugees throughout the day. They soon stopped bringing the refugees to Saigon, because the capital city was already jammed. Instead, the fleeing Vietnamese from farther north were taken to Camranh Bay on the coast of the South China Sea, where they had some chance of escaping by boat.

The last plane from Nhatrang was a Bird Air DC-6. After packing refugees into the aircraft, the crew could not get the door shut because of the press of humanity. The copilot pushed and shoved and socked to get the mob away from the door, but once the door was closed, the steps could not be moved. A crew chief climbed down a rope from the cockpit, shoved his way to the boarding steps and towed them away by jeep. Then he ran back to the rope and tried to climb up to the cockpit. As the crew above pulled him up, the mob tore off his pants and tried to climb up his body. Finally he was pulled free and into the cockpit and the plane started moving forward. But the mob refused to move back; some desperate Vietnamese threw themselves into the propellers as the craft finally made its getaway. "It was absolute chaos," Bird said.

In Saigon, the collapse was so quick that none of the evacuation plans carefully designed years earlier could be put into action. Bill Bird was in the Air America operations room when enemy bombers appeared overhead. Five-hundred-pound bombs shook the ground. A Bird Air C-130 was about to land, but Bird radioed it to stay away. On the ground was Bird's personal twin-engined Beech Bonanza. He had contracted to fly out a National Broadcasting Company television news crew, and in the late afternoon, soon after the bombing began, the NBC crew raced into Tan Son Nhut and announced that they were ready to leave.

Enemy rockets were raining down on the field, and Bird went outside to see if his Bonanza had been damaged. But he soon turned back. The taxiway was swarming with refugees on motorbikes, frantically seeking an escape from the crumbling South Vietnamese capital. "People were shooting at each other," Bird recalled later, "and at anything that moved." Bird advised the NBC crew that their departure would be delayed until dawn. Then he broke out a supply of Army field rations and cold beer.

Rockets continued to fall through the night, but at daybreak, Bird called the control tower and was told that all was quiet on the field. He informed the air controllers that the Bonanza was about to take off. It was a seven-seat aircraft, but 12 people managed to squeeze on board. Bird stayed behind, watching anxiously as the small plane roared down the runway and lifted safely into the air.

The field did not remain quiet for long. Rocket fire resumed later in the morning, making takeoffs and landings more and more hazardous. A South Vietnamese C-119 gunship got off the field successfully, and Bird watched as it tracked down a surface-to-air missile launcher team that had been creating havoc with aircraft using the field. The gunship made a slow 360-degree turn, spraying heavy fire into the launch crew. But one SA-7 missile that came snaking up found its way into one of the plane's engine pipes, and the C-119 turned into a ball of flame.

Another plane, a C-130, was already burning on the ramp. Half a minute later a second one exploded, then a third.

The end was clearly coming, and Bird decided it was time to leave. There was a United States Marine Corps helicopter taking on staffers from the command post at Tan Son Nhut. Bird got aboard and was lifted offshore to a United States Navy vessel lying in the South China Sea, part of a vast flotilla that was gathering evacuees from the falling city. The last few hours of the day were full of chattering helicopters poising over rooftops to collect the last escapees. And then Saigon fell.

The Communist victory in Vietnam marked the end of the long Indochina wars, and it seemed to signal the end, too, of an era of freelance flying that had captivated the popular imagination since the days of the Lafayette Escadrille and the Flying Tigers. Temporarily, at least, adventure-seeking pilots had to be content with more prosaic work in the service of Middle Eastern oil sheiks or out-of-the-way bush airlines; others went into the sordid world of drug smuggling. But flying mercenaries had turned to such peacetime pursuits in the past, only to be summoned to some new conflict that called for the singular blend of skill and daring that only they could offer. In time, no doubt, there would be other wars and other jobs for aerial soldiers of fortune.

An Air America helicopter full of Vietnamese refugees prepares to touch down aboard a United States Navy vessel in the South China Sea.

Acknowledgments

The index for this book was prepared by Gale Linck Partoyan. For their valuable help with the preparation of this volume, the editors thank: **In Belgium:** Brussels—Eric David, Brussels University; Anne Maaschalk. **In Denmark:** Vedbaek—Pastor Viggo Mollerup. **In Finland:** Helsinki—Lieutenant Colonel Erkki Heinliä (Ret.), Finnish Air Force; Lieutenant Colonel Risto Pajara (Ret.), Finnish Air Force. **In France:** Mesnil-Guyon—Jean Zumbach; Paris—Marianne de Fleury, Musée du Cinéma Henri Langlois; André Bénard, Odile Benoist, Elisabeth Bonhomme, Alain Degardin, Georges Delaleau, Gilbert Deloizy, Yvan Kayser, Général Pierre Lissarague, Director, Jean-Yves Lorent, Stéphane Nicolaou, Général Roger de Ruffray, Deputy-Director, Colonel Pierre Willefert, Curator, Musée de l'Air; Colonel Edmond Petit, Curator, Musée Air-France; Toulouse—Patrick P. Laureau. **In Great Britain:** London—Gerard Howson; Edna Lumb; Christopher Shores; Terence Spencer; Marjorie Willis, BBC Picture Library; Swindon—Brian Bridgeman. **In Israel:** Jerusalem—Israel Air Force; Israel Government Press Office. **In Italy:** Rimini—Nicola Malizia; Rome—Countess Maria Fede Caproni, Museo Aeronautico Caproni di Taliedo; Nino Arena. **In Mexico:** Mexico City—Jose Villela Gomez; Adolf Villasenor. **In Spain:** Algorta—Luis Ignacio de Azola Reyes; Barcelona—Asociación de Aviadores de la Republica; María Capdevila, Director, Fundacion Figueres; Dr. José Luis Infiesta Perez; Madrid—Pilar Colar, Editor, Ediciones Urbión; Rufo Gamazo, Director, Social Communications Media of the State; Manuel González; Colonel Jesús Salas de Larrazábal, Member of Joint Chiefs of Staff, Defense Ministry; Colonel Emilio Dáneo Palacios, Chief of the Office of Information, Dissemination and Public Relations of the Air Force Headquarters, Spanish Air Force; Javier de Juan y Penalosa, Publisher, Ediciones Urbión; Captain Ramón Hidalgo Salazar, Spanish Air Force; Sabadell—Juan Romeu Moratonas. **In Sweden:** Bromma—Countess Gunvor von Rosen; Malmo—Bertil Rubin, AB Text Och Bilder; Stockholm—Count Eric von Rosen. **In the United States:** In California—William Bird; Dick Rossi; Bill Blackbeard, Barbara Tiger, San Francisco Academy of Comic Art; Eric Shilling; R. T. Smith; John Underwood; Colonel John M. Williams, San Diego Aero-Space Museum; In Massachusetts— Victor Berch; In Nevada—James Hinds; In Texas—Richard Estrada; David Lee Hill; In Virginia—Charles Mott. Particularly useful sources of information and quotations used in this volume were: Biographic Files, National Air and Space Museum, Smithsonian Institution, Washington, D.C.; *Air America* by Christopher Robbins, G. P. Putnam's Sons, 1979; *The Nigerian Civil War* by John de St. Jorre, Hodder and Stoughton, London, 1972; *Some Still Live: Experiences of a Fighting-plane Pilot in the Spanish War* by F. G. Tinker, Lovat Dickson, London, 1938.

Bibliography

Books

Arnold, H. H., *Global Mission*. Harper & Brothers, 1949.

Bowers, Peter M., *Curtiss Aircraft: 1907-1947*. London: Putnam, 1979.

Chennault, Anna, *Chennault and the Flying Tigers*. Paul S. Eriksson, Inc., 1963.

Christy, Joe, and Jeff Ethell, *P-40 Hawks at War*. London: Ian Allan, 1979.

Francillon, René, *Japanese Aircraft of the Pacific War*. London: Putnam, 1970.

Goulart, Ron, *The Adventurous Decade*. Arlington House Publishers, 1975.

Hall, Bert, and John J. Niles, *One Man's War: The Story of the Lafayette Escadrille*. London: John Hamilton Limited, 1929.

Hempstone, Smith, *Rebels, Mercenaries, and Dividends: The Katanga Story*. Frederick A. Praeger, 1962.

Hoare, Mike, *Congo Mercenary*. London: Robert Hale, 1967.

Holtz, Robert, ed.:
Way of a Fighter: The Memoirs of Claire Lee Chennault. G. P. Putnam's Sons, 1949.
With General Chennault: The Story of the Flying Tigers. Coward-McCann, 1943.

Horn, Maurice, ed., *The World Encyclopedia of Comics*. Chelsea House Publishers, 1976.

July, Robert W., *A History of the African People*. Charles Scribner's Sons, 1970.

Karolevitz, Robert F., and Ross Fenn, *Flight of Eagles: The Story of the American Kosciuszko Squadron in the Polish-Russian War, 1919-1920*. Brevet Press, Inc., 1974.

Larrazábal, Jesús Salas de, *Air War Over Spain*. London: Ian Allan, 1969.

Madsen, Axel, *Malraux: A Biography*. William Morrow & Co., 1976.

Meyer, Karl E., and Tad Szulc, *The Cuban Invasion: The Chronicle of a Disaster*. Frederick A. Praeger, 1962.

Michalczyk, John J., *André Malraux's Espoir: The Propaganda/Art Film and the Spanish Civil War*. Romance Monographs, 1977.

Mockler, Anthony, *The Mercenaries*. The Macmillan Company, 1969.

Mok, Michael, *Biafra Journal*. Time-Life Books, 1969.

Nalty, Bernard C., *Tigers over Asia*. Elsevier-Dutton, 1978.

Nowarra, Heinz J., and G. R. Duval, *Russian Civil and Military Aircraft 1884-1969*. London: Fountain Press, 1970.

Nugent, John Peer, *The Black Eagle*. Stein and Day, 1971.

Parson, Edwin C., *I Flew with the Lafayette Escadrille*. Arno Press, 1972.

Robbins, Christopher, *Air America*. G. P. Putnam's Sons, 1979.

St. Jorre, John de, *The Nigerian Civil War*. London: Hodder and Stoughton, 1972.

Thayer, George, *The War Business: The International Trade in Armaments*. Simon and Schuster, 1979.

Thomas, Hugh, *The Spanish Civil War*. Harper & Row, 1977.

Tinker, F. G., *Some Still Live: Experiences of a Fighting-plane Pilot in the Spanish War*. London: Lovat Dickson, 1938.

Tuchman, Barbara W., *Stilwell and the American Experience in China, 1911-1945*. Macmillan Publishing Co., 1971.

Wise, David, and Thomas B. Ross, *The Invisible Government*. Random House, 1974.

Wyden, Peter, *Bay of Pigs: The Untold Story*. Simon and Schuster, 1979.

Periodicals

"Aeroplanes in the Balkans." *Aeronautics*, December 1913.

Brown, David A., "Turbo-Porter Displays Exceptional STOL." *Aviation Week and Space Technology*, October 5, 1964.

Cynzk, Jerzy B., "Kosciuszko Squadron." *Air Pictorial*, September 1965.

Herr, Allen, "American Pilots in the Spanish Civil War." *Journal of American Aviation Historical Society*, Fall 1977.

Jones, Ernest, "The Air War in Mexico." *Chirp*, December 1940.

"Of Chaika and Chato . . . Polikarpov's Fighting Biplanes." *Air Enthusiast 11*, November 1979-February 1980.

Scarborough, Bill, "Whitey Dahl's Luck Couldn't Last." *Climax*, October 1957.

Smith, Richard K., "Rebel of '33." *Shipmate* (U.S. Naval Academy Alumni Assn.), March 1977.

"Sweden's Muscular Minimus: The Saab Supporter-Safari." *Air International*, January 1975.

Picture credits

Index